The Empire of Love

By

W. J. DAWSON

ISBN - 978-93-5478-731-7

Design and setting By
Zinc Read
Email- zincread@gmail.com

Contents

I 1
II 6
III 11
IV 17
V 22
VI 27
VIII 35
IX 42
X 48
XI 54
XII 60
XIII 68
XIV 78

I
THE GENIUS TO BE LOVED

In the history of the last two thousand years there is but one Person who has been, and is supremely loved. Many have been loved by individuals, by groups of persons, or by communities; some have received the pliant idolatries of nations, such as heroes and national deliverers; but in every instance the sense of love thus excited has been intimately associated with some triumph of intellect, or some resounding achievement in the world of action. In this there is nothing unusual, for man is a natural worshipper of heroes. But in Jesus Christ we discover something very different; He possessed the genius to be loved in so transcendent a degree that it appears His sole genius.

Jesus is loved not for anything that He taught, nor yet wholly for anything that He did, although His actions culminate in the divine fascination of the Cross, but rather for what He was in Himself. His very name provokes in countless millions a reverent tenderness of emotion usually associated only with the most sacred and intimate of human relationships. He is loved with a certain purity and intensity of passion that transcends even the most intimate expressions of human emotion. The curious thing is that He Himself anticipated this kind of love as His eternal heritage with men. He expected that men would love Him more than father or mother, wife or child, and even made such a love a condition of what He called discipleship. The greatest marvel of all human history is that this prognostication has been strictly verified in the event. He is the Supreme Lover, for whose love, unrealizable as it is by touch, or glance, or spoken word, or momentary presence, men and women are still willing to sacrifice themselves, and surrender all things. The pregnant words of Napoleon, uttered in his last lonely reveries in St. Helena, still express the strangest thing in universal history: "Caesar, Charlemagne, I, have founded empires. They were founded on force, and have perished. Jesus Christ has founded an empire on love, and to this day there are millions ready to die for Him."

Napoleon felt the wonder of it all, the baffling, inexplicable marvel. Were we able to detach ourselves enough from use and custom, to survey the movement of human thought from some lonely height above the floods of Time, as Napoleon in the high sea-silences of St. Helena, we also might feel the wonder of this most wonderful thing the world has ever known.

That the majority of men, and even Christian men, do not perceive that the whole meaning of the life of Christ is Love is a thing too obvious to demand evidence or invite contradiction. I say men, and Christian men, thus limiting my statement, because women and Christian women, frequently do perceive it, being themselves the creatures of affection, and finding in affection the one sufficing symbol of life and of the universe. It is a St. Catherine who thinks of herself as the bride of Christ, and dreams the lovely vision of the changed hearts—the heart of Jesus placed by the hands that bled beneath her pure bosom, and her heart hidden in the side of Him who died for her. It is a St. Theresa who melts into ecstasy at the brooding presence of the heavenly Lover, and can only think of the Evil One himself with commiseration as one who cannot love. It is true that Francis of Assisi also thought and spoke of Christ with a lover's ecstasy, but then Francis in his exquisite tenderness of nature, was more woman than man. No such thought visited the stern heart of Dominic, nor any of those makers of theology who have built systems and disciplines upon the divine poetry of the divine Life.

Love, as the perfect symbol of life and the universe, does not content men, simply because for most men love is not the key to life, nor an end worth living for in itself, nor anything but a complex and often troublesome emotion, which must needs be subordinated to other faculties and qualities, such as greed, or pride, or the desire of power, or the dominant demands of intellect. Among men the poets alone have really understood Jesus: and in the category of the poets must be included the saints, whose religion has always been interpreted to them through the imagination. The poets have understood; the theologians rarely or never. Thus it happens that men, being the general and accepted interpreters of Christ, have all but wholly misinterpreted Him. The lyric passion of that life, and the lyric love which it excites, has been to them a disregarded music. They have rarely achieved more than to tell us what Christ taught; they have wholly failed to make us feel what Christ was. But Mary Magdalene knew this, and it was what she said and felt in the Garden that has put Christ upon the throne of the world. Was not her vision after all the true one? Is not a Catherine a better guide to Jesus than a Dominic? When all the strident theologies fall silent, will not the world's whole worship still utter itself in the lyric cry,

Jesu, Lover of my soul,
Let me to Thy bosom fly.

Is it then not within the competence of man to interpret Christ aright, simply because the masculine temperament is what it is? By no means, for such a statement would disqualify the evangelists themselves, who are the only biographers of Jesus. But in the degree that a temperament is only masculine, it will fail to understand Jesus. Napoleon could not understand; he was the child of force, the son of the sword, the very type of that hard efficiency of will and intellect which turns the heart to flint, and scorns the witness of the softer intuitions. Francis could understand because he was in part feminine—not weakly so, but nobly, as all poets and dreamers and visionaries are. Paul could understand for the same reason, and so could John and Peter; each, in varying degrees, belonging to the same type; but Pilate could not understand, because he had been trained in the hard efficiency of Rome; nor Judas, because the masculine vice of ambition had overgrown his affections, and deflowered his heart. What is it then in Paul and John and Peter, what element or quality, which we do not find in Pilate, Judas, or Napoleon? Clearly there is no lack of force, for the personality of these three first apostles lifted a world out of its groove and changed the course of history. Was it not just this, that each had beneath his masculine strength a feminine tenderness, a power of loving and of begetting love in others? John lying on the bosom of Jesus in sheer abandonment of love and sorrow at the last Supper; Peter, plunging naked into the Galilean sea, and struggling to the shore at the mere suspicion that the strange figure outlined there upon the morning mist is the Lord; Paul praying not only to share the wounds of Jesus, but if there be any pang left over, any anguish unfulfilled, that this anguish may be his—these are not alone immortal pictures, but they are revelations of a temperament, the temperament that understands Jesus. He who could not melt into an abandonment of grief and love over one on whom the shadow of the last hour rested; he who would spring headlong into no estranging sea to reach one loved and lost and marvellously brought near again; he who can share the festal wine of life, but has no appetite for agony, no thirsting of the soul to bear another's pain—these can never understand Jesus. They cannot understand Him, simply because they cannot understand love.

WHAT IS CHRISTIANITY?

TOWARDS GALILEE

The great obdurate world I know no more,
The clanging of the brazen wheels of greed,
The taloned hands that build the miser's store,
The stony streets where feeble feet must bleed.
No more I walk beneath thy ashen skies,
With pallid martyrs cruelly crucified
Upon thy predetermined Calvaries:
I, too, have suffered, yea, and I have died!
Now, at the last, another road I take
Thro' peaceful gardens, by a lilted way,
To those low eaves beside the silver lake,
Where Christ waits for me at the close of day.
Farewell, proud world! In vain thou callest me.
I go to meet my Lord in Galilee.

II
WHAT IS CHRISTIANITY?

Christianity, as it exists to-day, is in the main a misrepresentation and a misinterpretation of Christ; not consciously indeed—if it were so the remedy would be easy; but unconsciously, which makes the remedy difficult. One need not stop to define Christianity, for there is only one sincere meaning to the word; it implies a *kind of life whose spirit and method reproduce as accurately as possible the spirit and the method of the life of Jesus*. It would seem that if this interpretation of the term be correct there could be no difficulty in adjusting even unconscious misinterpretation of Christ to the true facts of the case: but here we are met by that perversity of vision which springs not from ignorance, but from thoughtlessness, and is in its nature much more obdurate than the worst perversity of ignorance. Ignorance can be enlightened; thoughtlessness, being usually associated with vanity, recognizes no need of enlightenment.

The life of Jesus, freshly introduced to a mind wholly ignorant of its existence may be trusted to convey its own impression; but the thoughtless mind will be either too proud, or too shallow, or too confident, to be sensitive to right impressions. Thus the trouble with most people who call themselves Christians is not to educate them into right conceptions of the life of Christ, but to destroy the growth of wrong impressions. "Surely," they will say, "we know all about the life of Christ. We have read the biographies of Jesus ever since the days of infancy. We have heard the life of Jesus expounded through long years by multitudes of teachers. We have a church which claims to have extracted from the life of Jesus a whole code of laws for life and conduct; is not this enough?" But what if the teachers themselves have never found the true secret of Jesus? What if they have but repeated the error of the Pharisees in elaborating a code of laws in which the vital spirit of the truth they would impart is lost? And does not the whole history of man's mind teach us that one simple truth known at first-hand is worth more to us, and is of greater influence on our conduct, than all the second-hand instruction we may receive from the most competent of teachers? It is just this first-hand thought which we most need. We need to see for ourselves what Jesus was, and not through the eyes of another, whatever his authority.

Suppose that we should read the Gospels in this spirit, with an entirely unbiassed and receptive mind, capable of first-hand impressions, what would be the probable character of these impressions? The clearest and deepest of all, I think, would be that the Jesus therein depicted lived His life on principles so novel that we are able to discover no life entirely like His in the best lives round about us. We should probably be struck first of all by certain outward dissimilarities. Thus He was not only poor, but He did not resent poverty—He beatified it. The things for which men naturally, and, as we think, laudably strive, such as a settled position in society and the consideration of others, He did not think worth seeking at all. He made no use of His abilities for private ends, which has been the common principle of social life since society began. He asked nothing of the world, being apparently convinced that nothing which the world could give Him was worth having. Strangest thing of all in one who must have been conscious of His own genius, and of the value of His teachings to mankind, He made not the least effort to perpetuate these teachings. He wrote no book, provided no biographer, did none of those things which the humblest man of genius does to ensure that distant generations shall comprehend and appreciate his character and message. He was content to speak His deepest truths to casual listeners. He spent all His wealth of intellect upon inferior persons, fishermen and the like, who did not comprehend one tithe of what He said. He was the friend of all who chose to seek His friendship. He discriminated so little that He even admitted a Judas to His intimacy, and allowed women tainted with dishonour and impurity to offer Him public tokens of affection. In all these things He differed absolutely from any other man who ever lived beneath the public eye. In all these things He still stands alone; for who, among the saintliest men we know, has not some innocent pride in his ability, or some preference in friendship, or some instinctive compliance with social usage, or some worldly hopes and honourable aims which he shares in common with the mass of men?

But these outward dissimilarities of conduct disclose a dissimilarity of soul. Men live for something; for what did Jesus live? And the answer that leaps upon us like a great light from every page of the Gospels is plain; He lived for love. If He did not care for praise or honour; if He regarded even the preservation of His teachings with a divine carelessness, it was because He had a nobler end in view, the love of men. He could not live without love, and His supreme aim was to make Himself loved. And yet it was less a conscious aim, than the natural working out of His own character. Fishermen by the sea saw Him but once; instantly they left their boats and followed Him. A man sitting at the receipt of custom, a hard man we should suppose, little likely to be swayed by sudden emotions, also sees Him once, and finds his occupation gone. A beautiful courtesan, beholding Him pass by, breaks from her lovers, and follows Him into an alien house, where she bathes His feet with tears and wipes them with the hairs of her head. Mature women without a word spoken or a plea made, minister to Him of their substance, and count their lives His. When He sleeps wearied out upon a rude fishing-boat, there is a pillow for His head, placed there by some unknown adorer. The men He makes apostles, all but one, count His smile over-payment for the loss of home, of wife, of children. Countless throngs of ordinary men and women forget their hunger, and are content to camp in desert places only to listen to the music of His voice. Wild and outlawed men, criminals and lepers and madmen, become as little children at His word, and all the wrongs and bruises inflicted on them by a cruel world are healed beneath His kindly glance. Does it matter greatly what He taught? This is how He lived. He lived in such a way that men saw that love was the only thing worth living for, that life had meaning only as it had love. And this is the imperishable tradition of Jesus:

This is His divinity,
This His universal plea,
Here is One that loveth thee.

What then is a true Christianity but the accurate reproduction of this spirit of love, the creation of loving and lovable men and women, who attract and uplift all around them by the subtle fascination of the love that animates them? What is a Christian Church but a confraternity of such men and women? What is a Christian society, but a society permeated by this spirit, and bringing all the affairs of life to its test? And what place have social superiorities and inferiorities; pride, scorn, or coldness; harsh theologies, breeding harsh tempers and infinite disputes; the egoism that wounds the humble, the strength that disregards the weak, the vanity that hurts the simple, in any company of men and women who dare to wear the name of such a Founder?

It was as a Bridegroom Christ came, anointed with all the perfumes of a dedicated love, and until the last bitter hour of His rejection, He moved with such lyric joyousness across the earth, that life became festive in His presence. It is as a Bride the church exists on earth, and if no festive smiles are awakened by its presence, and no gracious unsealing of the founts of love in human hearts, then is it not Christ's Church, for He has passed elsewhere with another company to the marriage-feast, and His Church stands without, before a barred and darkened door.

THE JUSTICE OF JESUS

HOW HE CAME

When the golden evening gathered on the shore of Galilee,
When the fishing boats lay quiet by the sea,
Long ago the people wondered, tho' no sign was in the sky,
For the glory of the Lord was passing by.

Not in robes of purple splendour, not in silken softness shod,
But in raiment worn with travel came their God,
And the people knew His presence by the heart that ceased to sigh
When the glory of the Lord was passing by.

For He healed their sick at even, and He cured the leper's sore,
And sinful men and women sinned no more,
And the world grew mirthful hearted, and forgot its misery
When the glory of the Lord was passing by.

Not in robes of purple splendour, but in lives that do His will,
In patient acts of kindness He comes still;
And the people cry with wonder, tho' no sign is in the sky,
That the glory of the Lord is passing by.

III
THE JUSTICE OF JESUS

One strong peculiarity of the teaching of Jesus—we might even call it its outstanding feature—is that it is frequently disclosed in a series of incidents. Unlike most teachers He philosophizes little about life. A single chapter of the Gospels, or at most two, would contain all the maxims about life which He thought necessary for wise and lofty conduct. His method is rather to put Himself in relation to the crucial occurrences of life, and to reveal the true way of regarding them by His own attitude towards them. When He would teach the beauty of humility it is by putting a little child in the midst of His arrogant and vainglorious disciples, that the child may become the living and memorable parable of His sentiments. When He would teach humanity, He does so by His own conduct to lepers. When He would discredit and expose the barbarism of the Mosaic Sabbatarian laws as interpreted by scribes and Pharisees, He does so by healing the sick and blind upon the Sabbath day. He is all for the concrete, teaching not by theory, but by example. The method is novel, and its advantages are obvious. The best conceived discourses on humility, mercy, or sympathy, might be forgotten, but no one can forget the child among the disciples, nor the raptured gaze of the blind man when his purged eyes open to behold the face of his miraculous Physician, nor the picture of Jesus touching without fear or disgust the leper whose unclean contagion made him an object of aversion even to the pitiful.

It is a wonderful method of instruction; it makes every other method seem trite and wearisome. Its effect is to make the Gospels a series of tableaux, which dwell in the memory as things actually seen. The groups upon the stage perpetually shift and rearrange themselves; each represents some phase of life, some problem, some combination of circumstance more or less common in the experience of men, something that is typical, for Jesus chooses only the typical and essential things of life for these occasions. The lesser things of life He passes over; it is the great and crucial matters which attract Him.

But what are the great things of life?

They all fall into one category, they all present problems in human relationship. No problems are so difficult. They are not speculative, but practical. A man who may be wise as the world counts wisdom, and able to pierce with acute analysis to the depth of the abstrusest philosophic problem, may nevertheless find himself hopelessly baffled by some quite common fact of life, such as how to treat a wayward son, or a sinful woman. I am not likely to lose a night's rest because I am unable to define the Trinity but with what sore travail of heart do I toss through midnight hours when I have to settle some course of action towards the friend who has betrayed me, the brother who has brought me shame, the child who scoffs at my restraint, and hears the call of the far country in every swift pulsation of his passionate heart! And why cannot I settle my course of action? Because my mind is confused by something which I call justice, to which custom has given authority and consecration. Justice prescribes one course of action, affection another. The convention of the world insists that wrong-doing should be punished, which is manifestly right; but when it insists that I should be the punisher, I suspect something wrong. The more closely I study conventional justice the more I am conscious of something in myself that distrusts and revolts from it. The more I incline to the voice of affection the more I fear it, lest I should be guilty of weakness which would merit my own contempt.

The struggle is one between convention and instinct, and I know not which side to take. But one thing I do know; it is that I have no certain clue to guide me, no clear determining principle that divides the darkness with a sword of light, no voice within myself that is authoritative.

Now the wonderful thing in Jesus is that He is always sure of Himself. Nothing takes Him by surprise, nothing produces the least hesitation in His judgment. Therefore He must have had an unfailing clue to which He trusted in the maze of life. Behind all consistency of judgment there must exist consistency of principle. The principle that governed all the thoughts of Jesus was *that love was the only real justice*. He came not to condemn, not to destroy men's lives, but to save them. There was no problem of human relationship that could not be solved by love; there was no other principle needed for the regulation of society; and no other could produce that general peace and good-will which He called the Kingdom of God.

Thus, on one occasion Jesus tells a story which is so lifelike in every touch that we may accept it, without doubt, as less a parable than an incident. A father has two sons, one of whom is industrious and dutiful, the other wayward and rebellious. The wayward son finally casts off all pretense of filial obedience, goes into a far country, and wastes his substance in riotous living. Here we have one of the saddest of all problems in human relationship, for presently the disgraced son comes home a beggar. The elder brother who represents the average social view, has no doubt whatever as to what should be done. He is offended that the disgraced son should come home at all; he would have thought better of him if he had hidden his shame in the country that had witnessed it. Probably his sense of pride and respectability is offended more than his love of virtue, though he characteristically gives his jealous anger the illusion of morality. This, I say, is the average social view. There are few things more cruel than affronted respectability. The elder brother is an eminently respectable person, totally unacquainted with wayward passions, and his only feeling for his brother is disdain.

Jesus tells the story, however, in such a way as to discredit the average social view. He begins by making us feel that whatever follies the prodigal had committed, he had already been punished for them in the miseries he had endured. It is not for man to punish with his whip of scorn one who has already been flaggellated with a whip of scorpions in the desert places of disgrace and shame. Jesus makes us feel also that whatever sins might be laid to the charge of the disgraced son, there is nevertheless in his heart a warmth of feeling of which the elder brother gives no sign. The boy loves his father, otherwise he would not have turned to him in his anguish of distress. The elder brother's attitude to his father is arrogant and harsh; the younger brother's is humble and tender. Lastly the father himself is revealed as the embodiment of love. He asks no questions, utters no reproaches, imposes no conditions; he simply takes his son back, in the rush of his affection cutting short the boy's pitiful confession, and calling for shoes and new robes and festal music, as though his son had returned in dignity and triumph. In the last scene of all, implied rather than described, the restored prodigal sits at the feast, leaning on his father's bosom, but the respectable son stands without in a darkness of his own creation—the darkness which a harsh spirit and an unlovely temper never fail to create in men of his unhappy temperament.

It is a very strange story, if we come to think of it; almost an immoral story, as no doubt it was considered by the Pharisees, and persons of their cold and mechanical type of virtue. But Jesus anticipates their criticism with one of the most startling statements that ever fell from inspired lips, "There is more joy in heaven among the angels of God over one sinner that repenteth than over ninety and nine righteous persons who need no repentance." Heaven approves the story, if they do not. Thus God Himself would act, for God is love. Thus love must needs act, if it be the kind of love that "suffereth long and is kind, doth not behave itself unseemly, seeketh not its own, is not provoked, taketh not account of evil, beareth all things, believeth all things, hopeth all things, endureth all things." And if we ask what becomes of justice, Jesus assures us that love is the only real justice. For the main object of justice is not punishment but reclamation. A truly enlightened justice is less concerned with the punishment of wrong than its reparation.

The gravest question in the case of this unhappy boy is not what he has made of himself by sin and folly, but what can yet be made of him by wise and tender treatment. Had the father coldly dismissed the prodigal with some bitter verdict on his past folly, he himself would have been unjust to the boy's possibilities, and thus would have sinned against his son with a sin much less capable of excuse than the son's sin against him. The worst sinner in the story is not the son who went wrong, but the son who had never done anything but right, yet had done it in such a way that it had begotten in him a vile, censorious, loveless temper. No one can be just who does not love; and so, once more removing the story into that unseen world which Christ called in to redress the balance of this visible world, we sinful men and women build our hopes upon the great saying that God's forgiveness is God's justice: if we confess our sins, He is not only faithful, but JUST in forgiving us our sins.

LOVE IS JUSTICE

THE WAY OF WOUNDS

He touched the leper tenderly,
So in His hands there came to be
  Wide wounds that were not wrought with nails.
Alas, my hands are smooth and fair,
No wound is on them anywhere,
  Nor any scarlet scar of nails.

His lips lay on the mouth of death,
God's healing dwelt within their breath,
  Wherefore his lips grew pale with pain,
And no man shall that pain divine;
Alas, my lips are red with wine,
  And they have scorned His draught of pain.

His feet were torn of stone and thorn,
Full slow He moved on roads forlorn,
  But joyous hearts accompanied Him;
Alas, my feet are softly shod,
And on the road that leads to God,
  They have not sought to move with Him.

And so all wounded by the way,
He came home at the close of day,
  And angels met Him at the Gate.
Alas, His way I have not known—
The road forlorn, the wounding stone—
  And no one waits me at the Gate.

IV
LOVE IS JUSTICE

Love is the only real justice—never was there a more revolutionary ethic! If Christianity is to be judged by its institutions, it must be reluctantly confessed that twenty centuries of Christian teaching have almost wholly failed to make this strange ethic acceptable to mankind. The elder brother still makes broad his phylacteries in the home, in the Church, and on the seat of justice. The elder brother's sense of offended respectability still masquerades as virtue. Who forgives as this father forgave, with such completeness that he who has wrought the wrong is encouraged to forget that the wrong was ever wrought? Where is the loving and tolerant spirit of the father less visible than in the Church, which crucifies men for a word, and makes a difference of opinion the ground for deadly enmity? Of what administration of law can we say that its chief object is not the punishment of the wrong-doer, but his reclamation? No existing society is organized on these principles, and the only defense the apologists of a bastard Christianity make is that it is totally impossible to apply the principles of Jesus to the administration of society. That is, at all events, an intelligible defense, but is it a legitimate one? Was Jesus merely a romantic dreamer, with entirely romantic views of love and justice? Was He a moral anarchist, whose teachings, if interpreted in laws, would destroy the basis of society? A strange thing indeed in human history if One who has been loved as no other was ever loved by multitudes of men and women through the ages, should prove after all to be an impracticable dreamer or a moral anarchist!

But if Jesus was a dreamer, He dreamed true, and the very reason why He is loved with such wide and deep devotion is that men do dimly, but instinctively, perceive that His life presents the only perfect pattern of life as it should be. Life, as it exists, is clearly not ordered on a social system which any wise or good man can approve. Hence the wise and good man is perpetually urged to the enquiry whether Jesus may not after all have been right?

Jesus certainly acts as one who is right. He acts always with the assured air of one for whom all debate is closed and henceforth impossible. He knows His way, and the great moral dilemmas of life yield instantly to His touch. He penetrates to their roots and makes us feel that He has touched the essential element in them. The dreamer vindicates himself by making it manifest that he sees deeper into the problem than the moralist, and that his is after all the better morality because it is of higher social value, and makes more directly for social reconciliation.

Let us take, for example, the judgment of Jesus upon the woman who was a sinner in the house of Simon the Pharisee. The social dilemma of the fallen woman is much more difficult of solution than that of the prodigal son. We expect a certain power of moral convalescence in youth which has been betrayed through folly. Sooner or later the manly nature kindles with resentment at its own weakness. Moreover, social law allows a certain opportunity of recuperation to man which it denies to woman. The sin of the woman seems less pardonable, not because it is worse in itself, but because it outrages a higher convention. Hence the strict moralist who might make some allowance for the hot blood of youth, makes none for woman when she is betrayed through the affections.

But this is the very point on which Jesus fixes as essential. "*The woman loved much, therefore let her many sins be forgiven,*" He says.

And a true reading of the story would seem to show that in uttering this sublime verdict Jesus is not thinking of the woman's sudden and pure love for Him; He is rather reviewing the entire nature of her life. She had loved much—that is her history in a sentence. Cruelty and unkindness, malice and bitterness, had no part in her misdoing. She had been undone through the very sweetness of her nature, as multitudes of women are. That which was her noblest attribute—her power of affection—had been the minister of her ruin through lack of wisdom and restraint. By love she had fallen, by love also she shall be redeemed. Her sins were indeed many, but behind all her sins there was an essential though perverted magnanimity of nature, and for the sake of an essential good in her, which lay like a shining pearl at the root of her debasement, she shall be forgiven.

Again a strange verdict, and one that must have seemed to the Pharisees entirely immoral. "What becomes of justice?" is their whispered comment. Jesus asserts His sense of justice by an exposition of the character of Simon. Simon is destitute of love, of magnanimity, even of courtesy. In his hard and formal nature there has been no room for emotion; passion of any kind and he are strangers. Which nature is radically the better, his or "this woman's"? Which presents the more hopeful field to the moralist? The soil of Simon's heart is thin and meagre; but in "this woman's" heart is a soil overgrown with weeds indeed, but delicately tempered, rich and deep, in which the roots of the fair tree of life may find abundant room and nourishment. Therefore she shall be forgiven for her possibilities, and such forgiveness is justice. To ignore these possibilities, to allow what she has been utterly to overshadow the lovely vision of what she may be, when once the soil is clear of weeds, and the real magnanimity of her temperament is directed into noble uses, would be the most odious form of injustice.

Such is the justice of Jesus, but, alas, after two thousand years we still stand astonished at it, more than half doubtful of its validity, and, if truth be told, secretly dismayed at its boldness. It is romantic justice, we say, but is it practicable justice? We might at least remember that what we call practicable justice has never yet attained the gracious results of Christ's romantic justice. Simon the Pharisee knows no more how to deal with "this woman" than the elder brother knew how to deal with the prodigal. Such sense of justice as they possessed would have infallibly driven the penitent boy back to the comradeship of harlots, and have refused the penitent harlot the barest chance of reformation. Is not this enough to make the least discerning of us all suspect that Pharisees and elder brothers, for all their immaculate respectability of life, are by no means qualified to pass judgment on these tragedies of life with which they have no acquaintance, and cannot have an understanding sympathy? Does not the entire failure of legal justice with all its apparatus of punishment and repression, to give the sinner a vital impulse to withdraw from his sin, drive us to the conclusion, or at least to the hope, that there must be some better method of dealing with sinners than is sanctioned by conventional justice? There is another method—it is Christ's method. And the thing to be observed is that whereas conventional justice must certainly have failed in either of these crucial instances, the romantic justice of Jesus—if we must so call it—completely succeeded. The woman who was a sinner sinned no more, and the penitent son henceforth lived a new life of purity and obedience. In each case love is justified, and proves itself the highest justice.

LOVE AND FORGIVENESS

LOVE'S PROFIT

What profits all the hate that we have known
  The bitter words, not all unmerited?
Have hearts e'er thriven beneath our angry frown?
Have roses grown from thistles we have sown?
  Or lucid dawns flowered out of sunsets red?
    Lo, all in vain
The violence that added pain to pain,
And drove the sinner back to sin again.

We had been wiser had we walked Love's way
  We had been happier had we tenderer been,
We had found sunlight in the cloudiest day
Had we but loved the souls that went astray,
  And sought from shame their many faults to screen
    Lo, they and we
Had thus escaped Life's worst Gethsemane,
And found the Garden where the angels be.

For One there was who, angry, drew no sword,
  Derided, wept for those who wrought Him wrong,
And at the last attained this great reward,
That those who injured Him acclaimed Him Lord,
  And wove His story into holiest song.
    So sinners wrought
For Him the Kingdom He had vainly sought,
And to His feet the world's frankincense brought.

V
LOVE AND FORGIVENESS

In these instances it is the singular completeness of Christ's forgiveness which is the most startling feature. It would be a libel on human nature to say that men do not forgive each other, but human forgiveness usually has reservations, reticences, conditions. Jesus taught unlimited forgiveness, and what He taught He practiced.

"Then came Peter, and said to Him, 'Lord, how oft shall my brother sin against me and I forgive him? Until seven times?' Jesus said unto him, 'I say not unto thee, until seven times; but until seventy times seven.'"

It is a vehement reply, in which a quiet note of scorn vibrates; not scorn of Peter, but scorn of any kind of love that is less than limitless. But whose love is limitless? Do we not commonly speak of love as being outworn by offense or neglect? In the compacts which we make with one another in the name of love, do we not specifically name certain offenses as unpardonable? Thus one man will say, "I can forgive anything but meanness," and another says, "no friendship can survive perfidy"; and in the relations between men and women unfaithfulness is held to cancel all bonds, however indissoluble they may seem. Now and again, it is true, some strange voice reaches us, keyed to a different music. Shakespeare, for example, in his famous one hundred and sixteenth sonnet, boldly states that

Love is not love
Which alters when it alteration finds,
Or bends with the remover to remove.

But who listens, who believes? Yet, if it should happen to us to be placed in the position of the offender, we need no one to convince us that a true love should be, in its very nature, unalterable. How astonished and dismayed are we, when eyes that have so many times met ours in tenderness harden at our presence, and lips which have uttered so many pledges of affection, speak harshly! We do not deny our fault, indeed; but we think we can discern reasons why it should be regarded mercifully, why the very memory and sacredness of old affection should make harsh judgment impossible; nay, more, why a deeply generous love should even rejoice in the opportunity to forgive, and so should sanctify our very shame with the healing touch of pity, and pour our tears into the sacramental cup which ratifies a new fidelity.

It is so the sinner argues, his vision of what love ought to be growing clearer by his offense against love. It is he alone, the sinner, who can really sympathize with Christ's conception of love, for he alone feels that this is the kind of love he needs. The elder brother does not understand, Simon the Pharisee does not understand, because neither has sinned in such a way as to be flung helpless at the feet of love. Peter did not understand when he put his question to Christ. He spoke just as the average man would speak, who has never sounded the tragic depths in life, has never known the misery of weakness, and therefore has no fellow feeling for the weak. Love as such men know it is less a passion than a compact. It is a bond of mutual advantage, guarded from abuse by swift penalty and forfeit. It is the reward of qualities, it gives no more than it gets, it exists by an equal equipoise of service. If this equipoise is disturbed its obligations are dissolved. It is easily affronted, and under affront becomes resentful, bitter, even vindictive. How oft shall I forgive my brother? Only as oft as a sense of duty shall demand, only up to the point which is sanctioned by social custom, so that I may save my reputation for magnanimity, always excepting certain sins for which no pardon can be legitimately asked. But the hour was not far off when Peter himself was to commit the very sins for which customary love has no pardon. He was to be guilty of those offenses which just and good men say they cannot forgive—meanness, cowardice, perfidy, denial. That bitter hour revealed the true nature of love to Peter. He knew that in spite of his sin against Jesus, he still loved Him, and since love was unalterable in him, he expected an unalterable love in Christ. It was the seventy times seven forgiveness that he needed then; and how sweet to recollect in that hour that Jesus had taught a love that knew no limit. "*Lovest thou Me*?" was the one word his Master uttered when they met in the quiet morning light beside the sea. "*Thou knowest all things, Thou knowest that I love Thee,*" was the swift reply. Storms disturb the sea but the central tides run on. Peter found with equal astonishment and gratitude that not even perfidy was able to separate him from the love of Christ, for that love was unalterable as the morning star which hung above the lake, and cleansing as the soft waves that lapped its shore.

The self-righteous man will never understand these things. Men and women of meagre natures, with whom love is a compact, not a passion, will vehemently disapprove them. People of smooth lives, ignorant of strong temptations, will refuse even to discuss them. Jesus was well aware of their implacable indifference or cold hostility, and boldly said that for such people He had no gospel. His mission was not to the whole, but to the sick. The Gospel of Jesus is in truth not designed for people of comfortable lives. He has little to say to the children of compromise, whose emasculated lives attain the semblance of virtue by the cautious exercise of niggard passions. They can take care of one another, these righteous ones, whose very righteousness is a negation.

But Christ's Gospel is for a tragic world. It is for the disinherited, the weak, and the strong who have become weak; for those who have been wrecked by folly and passion, and too much love of living; for those whose capacities for good and evil, being both rooted in passion, are equally a peril and a potency—it is to these Christ chiefly speaks. To them the Gospel of unlimited forgiveness and unalterable love is the only vital, because the only efficacious Gospel. The man whose very virility of nature makes him the easy prey of murderous joy; the man shut up in prison, who hears from the lips that once spake love to him, the sentence of inexpiable disgrace; the outcast from honour, gnawing the bitter husks of hated sin in far lands, and tortured in his dreams by the sweetness of recollected happiness; these, and all like these, will understand Jesus, for it is to them He speaks. Their very sin interprets Him. To their forlorn ears the love He teaches will sound not strange, for it is the only kind of love that can redeem them; nor foolish, for it is the only love that dare stoop low enough to lift them up. These will not fail to understand what conventional righteousness finds so difficult; these, and also all good women who have had acquaintance with either deep love or real grief, because it is a loving woman's sweet prerogative and divine disposition to forgive, and to draw from her grace of forgiveness a more tender and maternal power of loving.

THE PRACTICE OF LOVE

FELLOW SUFFERERS

When men of malice wrought the crown for Thee
Didst Thou complain?

Nay; in each thorn God's finger Thou didst see,
 His love thro' pain.

His finger did but press the ripened Vine,
 Thy fruit to prove,
That henceforth all the world might drink the wine
 Of Thy great love.

So when the darkness rose about Thy feet
 Thy lips met His,
Amid the upper light, in Death's long sweet,
 Releasing kiss.

And shall I cry aloud in anger when
 Men make for me
A Cross less harsh? Nay, I'll remember then
 Thy constancy.

And if the darkness hide me from Thy sight
 At God's command,
I'll talk with Thee all thro' the prayerful night,
 And touch Thy hand;

Greatly content, if I whose life has been
 So long unwise,
May, wounded, on Thy wounded bosom lean
 In Paradise.

VI
THE PRACTICE OF LOVE

So convinced was Jesus that love alone was the master law of life, that He based His own life wholly on His conviction, cheerfully accepting all the risks which were implied. He was perfectly aware of the consequences to Himself and His reputation when He made Himself the friend of publicans and sinners. These consequences He ignored, making Himself of no reputation, that He might uplift by His love those who needed His love the most. Under the constant contradiction of those who mistook His spirit, and even libelled His character, He manifested neither bitterness nor resentment. He suffered injuries without retaliation, and went so far as to denounce all forms of retaliation as a wasteful expenditure of spirit, wrong in themselves, and attaining no end but the worse injury of those who employed them. He might easily have used the miraculous power which He possessed for His own defense, and for the confusion of His enemies. Had He been selfishly ambitious, He might have organized a party so strong, that it would have become an irresistible force, which would have shattered the old order whose evils He denounced, and have made Him the dictator of a new order, based on the ideals in which He believed. He did none of these things, not through lassitude of spirit or failure to perceive their possible issues, but simply because these were not the things to do. In His judgment the only abiding kingdom belonged to the meek. He who suffered injustice with patience would prove the ultimate conqueror. There was an irresistible might in love and meekness against which the people raged in vain. Love was a working and practicable law of life; in the long issue of things it was the only law that justified itself.

Was Jesus right in these conclusions? Can human life proceed along the lines He indicated? Certainly it has never yet done so. The woman who is a sinner finds no Jesus to absolve her utterly among the priests of His religion. The resentment of injury is regarded even by good men as entirely justified when injury to the person involves the rights of social order. Force is regarded by persons of the highest amiability as necessary to the defense of society, and the Church applauds the punishments inflicted by the civil magistrate, and even hastens to bless the banners and baptize the deadly weapons of the warrior. Meekness, which endures injury without resentment, is regarded as the sign of a servile and cowardly spirit, and is the subject of ridicule and contempt. No Christian society exists in which a Peter would be freely pardoned his offense; the best that could be hoped would be the infliction of humiliating penance, and a reluctant reinstatement in the apostleship after a long period of bitter ostracism. Yet who would venture to challenge the conduct of Jesus in these respects? Who would not find his opinion of Jesus tragically lowered, and his adoration practically destroyed, if some new and more authentic Gospel were discovered by which we learned that Jesus smote with leprosy the Pharisees who resisted Him, as Elisha smote Gehazi: that He sanctioned the stoning of the adultress taken in the act of sin; or that He branded Simon Peter for his perfidy, and drove him out forever from the apostleship he had disgraced, denouncing him as a son of hell and a predestined citizen of the outer darkness? Could such acts be attributed to Jesus, though each act in itself would precisely represent the common temper of Christian courts and so-called Christian men under circumstances of similar and equal provocation, the worship of Jesus would at once cease throughout the world.

The dilemma is truly tragic. A Jesus who should be proved to have lived according to the conventions we respect, who did not rise above conventional ideals of either love or justice, who approved force, and resented injuries, who repudiated the friend who had betrayed Him, who shunned the contact of persons whose touch dishonoured Him—such a Jesus would cease to be our Jesus. He would no longer attract us, He would not touch our hearts, He would barely command our respect. Astounding fact! Those very things in the life of Jesus which we disapprove are the things for which we love Him; and those tempers which we ourselves disallow are in Him the sources of our adoration.

We are bound therefore to ask, can that method of conduct be wrong which has won this triumphant issue? It may be ironically true that we love Him most for those very acts of His which we are least likely to imitate; but is not this our tacit testimony to the essential rightness of these acts? In our better, or our softer moments; or in those moments when we are most conscious of the cruelty of life, and most in need of love, do we not feel, as the life of Jesus grows before us, that this is how life should be lived? Dare we question that a world governed wholly by the ideals of Jesus would be a far happier world than this we know? Love, as the one necessary law of life, clearly stands justified in Jesus, since it has produced the most adorable character in history. If we admit this, it is foolish to speak of Christ's ideals as impracticable. What we approve in another's life we cannot wholly repudiate in our own. Let it be added also, that a life lived by another is always a life that others can live. We may seek to cover our failure, and the world's failure, to reproduce the life of Jesus, by the plea of incompetence, but against our plea Jesus records His verdict, "*Behold I have left you an example.*"

From that verdict there is no appeal.

LOVE AND JUDGMENT

MOTHER AND SON

When, for the last time, from His Mother's home
The Son went forth, foreseeing perfectly
What doom would happen, and what things would come,
Was there upon His lips no stifled sigh
For happy hours that should return no more,
Long days among the lilies, pure delights
Of wanderings by Galilee's fair shore,
And converse with His friends on starry nights?
Yet brave He stepped into the setting sun
With this one word, "Father, Thy will be done!"

With a low voice the stooping olive-trees
Whispered to Him of His Gethsemane;
The cruel thorn-bush, clinging to His knees,
Proclaimed, "I shall be made a crown for Thee!"
And, looking back, His eyes made dim with loss,
He saw the lintel of the cottage grow
In shape against the sunset, like a cross,
And knew He had not very far to go.
Yet brave He stepped into the setting sun,
Still saying this one word, "Thy will be done!"

So, when the last time, from His Mother's home
The Son passed out, no choir of angels came,
As long before at Bethlehem they had come,
To comfort Him upon the road of shame.
Alone He went, and stopped a little space,
As one overburdened, stopped to look again
Upon His Mother's pleading form and face,
And wept for her, that she should know this pain.
Then, silently, He faced the setting sun
And said, "Oh, Father, let Thy will be done!"

VII

LOVE AND JUDGMENT

Just as Jesus called in the vision of the unseen world to redress the balance of the visible world, when He said that there was more joy in heaven over the penitent sinner than over ninety and nine just men who needed no repentance, so in His final addresses to His followers He again discloses the unseen world. These final addresses deal with the tremendous problem of a future judgment. Over no problem does the human mind hover with such breathless interest, such unfeigned alarm. But with characteristic perversity the elements in Christ's vision of the judgment on which men have seized most tenaciously, are precisely those elements which are least intelligible, and least capable of strict definition. It is around the word "eternal" and the nature of the punishment suggested, that the theological battles of centuries have centred. Yet the really central point of both the vision and the teaching, is not here at all; and it is only man's habitual love of enigma which can explain the passion with which men have opposed one another over the interpretation of words and phrases which must always remain enigmatic.

Let us turn to Christ's vision of the Judgment, as recorded by St. Matthew, and what do we find? First that the same Son of Man, whose whole life was an exposition of the law of love, is Himself the final judge of men and nations. "*The Son of Man shall sit on the throne of His glory, and before Him shall be gathered all the nations, and He shall separate them one from another, as the shepherd separates the sheep from the goats.*" No alien judge, observe, unacquainted with the nature of man, but one who knows human life so thoroughly that He is the representative man—"the Son of Man";

and although He is now the Judge, yet He still calls Himself by the tender name of the Shepherd. The tribunal is therefore the tribunal of love, and the court is the court of love. He who shall judge mankind is He who judges Peter and the woman who was a sinner, He of whose tenderness and sympathy we have assurance in a hundred acts of mercy, pity, and magnanimity. Yet for centuries the Church has sung its terrible *Dies Irae*, has clothed the judgment seat with thunder, has put into the hands of Jesus bolts of flame, and has applauded and enthroned in His sanctuaries such pictorial blasphemies as Michael Angelo's *Last Judgment*, which represents Jesus as an angry Hercules, and even gratifies the private spite of the artist by overwhelming in a sea of fire one who had offered him a personal affront.

Blasphemy indeed, and falsehood too; for the second thing we find is that the one principle which governs the entire vision of Jesus is that Love judges, and that it is by Love that men are tested. The men and women of loving disposition, who have wrought many little acts of kindness which were to them so natural and simple that they do not so much as recollect them, find themselves mysteriously selected for infinite rewards. The men and women of opposite disposition, in spite of all their outward rectitude of behaviour, find themselves numbered with the goats. A cup of cold water given to a child, a meal bestowed upon a beggar, a garment shared with the naked—these things purchase heaven. One who Himself had been thirsty, hungry, and naked, judges their worth, and He judges by His own remembered need. It is love alone that is divine, love alone that prepares the soul for divine felicity. With a beautiful unconsciousness of any merit, the people who have lived lovingly plead ignorance of their own lovely acts and tempers; but they have been witnessed by the hierarchies of heaven, the morning stars have sung of them, they have made glad the heart of God; and the reward of these humble servitors of love now is that having added to the joy of God, henceforth they shall share that joy forever.

Never was there vision at once so exquisite and so surprising. It is like a child's dream of heaven and judgment, so untouched is it by the conventions of the world, so innocent, so daring, so tenderly imagined, and so impossibly probable. Alas, that most of us are too wise to understand it, and too worldly to receive it. Yet in nothing that Jesus uttered is there clearer evidence of deliberation. And it is of a piece with all He taught; so much so indeed that without it, His teaching would be incomplete.

Truly, we may say, the Heaven of Jesus is a strangely ordered Kingdom; for in it beggars are comforted for apparently no other reason than that they need comfort; the doers of forgotten kindnesses are crowned with sudden splendours of divine approval while the lords of genius and the makers of empire are forgotten; and the very anthems of the blessed are hushed into silent wondering and joy when solitary penitents turn homewards from the roads of sin! But it is not stranger than that kingdom in which Jesus lived habitually, the kingdom He created round Him in His earthly life. In that kingdom also love was lord, and she who anointed the tired feet of the Master against His burial was promised everlasting remembrance, and she who out of her penury gave her mite to the poor was praised as having done more than all the rich, who from their abundance distributed careless and unmissed benefactions. In all that Jesus says and does the same sequence of thought runs clear, the same master principle rules the various result. Life is a unity either here or hereafter, and love is, and must evermore remain, the one temper that gives significance to life.

THE WISDOM OF THE SIMPLE

THE WELL

When Galilee took morning's flame
Thro' fields of flowers the Master came.
He stopped before a cottage door,
And took from humble hands the store
Of crumbs that from the table fell,
And water from the living well.
He smiled, and with a great content
Upon the road of flowers went.

Foredoomed upon the road of shame
With bleeding feet the Master came,
And found the cottage door again.
"No wine have we to ease Thy pain,
But only water in a cup."
The Master slowly drank it up.
"Thy kindness turns it into wine,"
He said, "and makes the gift divine."

Upon a day the Master trod
The road of stars that leads to God,
All tasks for men accomplished.
"They gave Me hate," He softly said,
"But Love in larger measure gave,
And therefore was I strong to save.
I had not reached the Cross that day
But for the Well beside the way."

VIII
THE WISDOM OF THE SIMPLE

If these things be true, if the whole tradition of Jesus is an exposition of love as the law of life, the deduction is entirely simple, and as logical as it is simple. That deduction has been already stated. It is that Christianity is a method of life by which men and women are taught and inspired to love as Jesus loved, and to live loving and lovable lives. It has little to do with creeds, and still less with formal codes of conduct. For this reason such a definition of Christianity will satisfy neither the theologian nor the philosopher. Jesus never expected that it would. He knew that the one would regard it as heretical, and the other as so deficient in subtlety as to seem foolish. Therefore He made His appeal to simple and natural people, saying that what was hidden from the wise and prudent, was revealed to babes.

The simple and natural people understood Jesus; they always do. The sophisticated and artificial people did not understand Him; they never will. With scarcely an exception the people of intelligence and culture regarded Him with disdain, withdrew from Him, or violently opposed Him. The reason for their conduct lay not so much in either their culture or their intelligence, as in the kind of life that seemed to be necessary to them as the expression of their culture.

Thus, they were full of prejudices, prepossessions, and foregone conclusions, all of which had the sanction of their culture. It was enough for them to know that Jesus came from Nazareth and was unlettered; this produced in them violent scorn and antipathy. They were still further offended because He used none of the shibboleths with which they were familiar. Nor could they conceive of any life as satisfactory but the kind of life they lived, and that was a life of social complexity, ruled by conventional usages and maxims, and essentially artificial in ideal and practice. Jesus, therefore, turned from them to the simple and natural people, fishermen, artisans, and humble women, in whom the natural instincts had fuller play. His reward was immediate; then, and ever since, the Common People heard Him gladly.

The reason why simple and natural people readily understand Jesus is that in the kind of life they live the primal emotions are supreme. The very narrowness of their social outlook intensifies those emotions. They have little to distract them; they are not bewildered by endless disquisitions on conduct, and religion itself is for them an emotion rather than a systematized creed. For the poor man home, children, fireside affection, mean more than for the rich man, because they are his only wealth. This is the lesson which Wordsworth has so nobly taught in his "*Song at the Feast of Brougham Castle,*"—

How, by heaven's grace this Clifford's heart was framed,
How he, long forced in humble walks to go,
Was softened into feeling, soothed and tamed.

Love had he found in huts where poor men lie;
His daily teachers had been woods and rills,
The silence that is in the starry sky,
The sleep that is among the lonely hills.

People who live thus, in wise simplicity, undistracted by the numerous illusions of an artificial life, have no difficulty in accepting Christ's teaching that love is the supreme law of life, because love means everything to them in the kind of life they lead. In the wisdom of the heart they are more learned than the wisest Pharisee, who is rarely "softened into feeling," whose whole social life indeed imposes a restraint on feeling. What peasant father would not welcome a returning prodigal, what peasant mother would not open her arms wide to gather to her bosom a penitent daughter, recovered from the cruel snare of cities? Certainly one is much more likely to find such acts of pure feeling among peasant folk than among the rich and cultured, for the peasant cares less for opinion, is less respectful of social etiquette, and follows more closely in his actions the instincts of primal affection. Who has not discovered among poor and humble folk a strange and beautiful lenience, the lenience of a great compassion, towards those sins which in more artificial conditions of society are held to justify the most violent condemnation, and do indeed close the heart to pity? In poor men's huts beside the Sea of Galilee Jesus Himself had found love, love in all its divine daring, lenience, and magnanimity, and He knew that among people like these He would be understood. He also knew that the only people fitted to interpret His doctrine of sovereign love to the world were these simple folk of the lake and field, and therefore to them He committed His Gospel, and from them He chose His disciples.

It needed a peasant Christ to teach these things, for no other could have imagined them, no other could have had the daring and simplicity to utter them. A peasant Christ He was, living, thinking, and acting as a peasant even in His highest moments of inspiration. It was because He always remained a peasant that He was able to see so clearly the defects of that more intricate social system to which His ministry introduced Him. He brought with Him a new scale of values, which He had learned in the school of a more primal life than could be found in cities. Nature always spoke in Him, convention never. In His treatment of sin it is always the voice of Nature that we hear triumphing over the verdicts of convention. The sins which convention regards as inexpiable are sins of passion; the sins which it excuses are sins of temper, such as greed, malice, craft, unkindness, cruelty. Jesus entirely reverses the scale. His pity is reserved for outcasts, His harshest words are addressed to those whom the world calls good. Folly He views with infinite compassion—the foolish man is as a lost sheep whose very helplessness invokes our pity. But for the man of hard and self-sufficient nature, whose very righteousness is a mixture of prudence and egoism, He has only words of flame. An offense against virtue counts for less with Him than an offense against love. No wonder the Pharisees called Him a blasphemer! Were the true nature of Christ's teaching understood to-day many who profess to revere Him would join in the same accusation. What more offensive and unpalatable truth could be presented to mankind than this on which Jesus constantly insists, that sins of temper are much more harmful than sins of passion, that they spring from a more incurable malignancy of nature, that they produce far wider and more disastrous suffering?

Yet the truth is clear enough to all broadly truthful and simple natures, which are not bewildered by conventional views of right and wrong. Who has occasioned more suffering, the youth who has sinned against himself in wild folly and repented, or the man who has planned his life with that cold craft and deliberate cruelty which sacrifices everything to self-advantage? Can any human mind measure the various and almost infinite wrongs committed by the man who piles up through years of sordid avarice an unjust fortune? Who can count the broken hearts in the pathway of that implacable ambition which "wades through slaughter to a throne"? These things may not be apparent to the man whose nature is subdued to the hue of that artificial society in which he lives, a society which permits such crimes to pass unquestioned. They are certainly not perceived by the criminals themselves. To-day, as in the day of Christ, they "devour widows' houses, and for a pretense make long prayers," save, perhaps, that more blind than the ancient Pharisees, their prayers seem real, and they themselves are unconscious of pretense. Now also, as then, they give their tithes in conventional benevolence, forgetting, and hoping to make others forget, the sources of their wealth in their use of it. How is it that such men are so unconscious of offense? Simply because they have never grasped Christ's deliberate statement that sins of temper are much worse than sins of passion; that cruelty is a worse thing than folly; that the wrong wrought by squandering the substance in a far country is more quickly repaired, and more easily forgiven, than the wrong of hoarding one's substance in the avarice which neglects the poor, or adding to it by methods which trample the weak and humble in the dust, as deserving neither pity nor attention.

Yet it needs but a very brief examination of society to prove the truth of Christ's contention; very little experience of life to discover that the utmost corruption of the human heart lies in lovelessness. The spiteful and rancorous temper, always seeking occasions of offense; the jealous spirit which cannot bear the spectacle of another's joy; the bitter nagging tongue, darting hither and thither like a serpent's fang full of poison, and diabolically skilled in wounding; the sour and grudging disposition, which seems most contented with itself when it has produced the utmost misery in others; the narrow mind and heart destitute of magnanimity; the cold and egoistic temperament, which demands subservience of others and receives their service without thanks, as though the acknowledgment of gratitude were weakness—these are common and typical forms of lovelessness, and who can estimate the sum of suffering they inflict? Their fruit is everywhere the same; love repressed, children estranged, the home made intolerable. It does but add to the offense of these unlovely people that in what the world calls morality they are above reproach, for they instill a hatred of morality itself by their appropriation of it. Before them love flies aghast, and the tenderest emotions of the heart fall withered. Could the annals of human misery be fairly written, it might appear that not all the lusts and crimes which are daily blazoned to the eye have wrought such wide-spread misery, have inflicted such general unhappiness, as these sins of temper, so common in their operation that they pass almost unrebuked, but so wide-spread in their effects that their havoc is discovered in every feature of our social life.

THE REVELATIONS OF GRIEF

THE HOUSE OF PRIDE

I lived with Pride; the house was hung
  With tapestries of rich design.
Of many houses, this among
  Them all was richest, and 'twas mine.
But in the chambers burned no fire,
  Tho' all the furniture was gold,
I sickened of fulfilled desire,
  The House of Pride was very cold.

I lived with Knowledge; very high
  Her house rose on a mountain's side.
I watched the stars roll through the sky,
  I read the scroll of Time flung wide.
But in that house, austere and bare,

No children played, no laughter clear
Was heard, no voice of mirth was there,
The House was high but very drear.

I lived with Love; all she possest
Was but a tent beside a stream.
She warmed my cold hands in her breast,
She wove around my sleep a dream.
And One there was with face divine
Who softly came, when day was spent,
And turned our water into wine,
And made our life a sacrament.

IX
THE REVELATIONS OF GRIEF

Nevertheless there are occasions in life when these things become evident to even the least observant of us. When we stand beside the newly dead the most intolerable reflection of countless mourners is that their tears fall on quiet lips to which they gave scant caresses, in the days of health: their passionate words of love are uttered to unhearing ears, which in life waited eagerly for such assurances as these, and waited vainly. All the purity and beauty of the vanished human soul is revealed to us now, when it is no longer in our power to gladden or delight it with our kindness or our praise. All the willing service rendered to us by those folded hands and resting feet, which we so thanklessly accepted, is seen as a thing dear and precious to us now, when the opportunity of thanks is past forever. What would we give now if but for one brief hour we might recall our dead just to say the tender things we might have said and did not say, through all those days and years when they were with us,—presences familiar and accustomed, moving round us with so soft a tread that we scarce regarded them, nor laid on them detaining hands, nor lifted our preoccupied and careless eyes to theirs!

For most of us, alas, it is not Grief and Love alone who conduct us to the chambers of the dead; the sad and silent Angel of Reproach also stands beside the bed, and the shadow of his wings falls upon the features fixed in their immutable appeal, their pathetic and unwilling accusation. Then it is that veil after veil is lifted from the past, till in the pitiless light we read ourselves with a new understanding of our faults. We see that through some element of hardness in ourselves which we allowed to grow unchecked; through vain pride, or obstinate perversity, or mere thoughtless disregard, we repulsed love from the dominion of our hearts, and made him the servitor of our desires, but no longer the lord of our behaviour and the spirit of our lives. And now as we gaze on these things across the gulf of the irreparable, we see our sin and how it came to pass; how we were unkind not in the things we did but in those we failed to do; how, without being cruel, our denied response to hearts that craved our tenderness became a more subtle cruelty than angry word or hasty blow; how with every duty accurately measured and fulfilled, yet love evaporated in the cold and cheerless atmosphere of repression and aloofness with which we clothed ourselves; and then the significance of Christ's teaching comes home to us, for we know too late, that kindness is more than righteousness, and tenderness more than duty, and that to have loved with all our hearts is the only fulfilling of the law which heaven approves. None, bowed beside the newly dead, ever regretted that they had loved too well; millions have wept the bitterest tears known to mortals because they loved too little, and wronged by their poverty of love the sacred human presences now withdrawn forever from their vision.

But there are other and more joyous ways of learning the truth of Christ's teaching, ways that are accessible to all of us. The best and most joyous way of all is to make experiment of it. Here is a law of life which to the sophisticated mind seems impossible, impracticable, and even absurd. No amount of argument will convince us that we can find in love a sufficient rule of life, or that "to renounce joy for our fellow's sake is joy beyond joy." How are we to be convinced? Only by making the experiment, for we really believe only that which we practice. "I wish I had your creed, then I would live your life," said a seeker after truth to Pascal, the great French thinker. "Live my life, and you will soon have my creed," was the swift reply. The solution of all difficulties of faith lies in Pascal's answer, which is after all but a variant of Christ's greater saying, "He that willeth to do the will of God, shall know the doctrine." Is not the whole reason why, for so many of us, the religion of Christ which we profess has so little in it to content us, simply this, that we have never heartily and honestly tried to practice it? We have accepted Christ's religion indeed, as one which upon the whole should be accepted by virtuous men, or as one which has sufficient superiorities to certain other forms of religion to turn the scale of our intellectual hesitation, and win from us reluctant acquiescence. But have we accepted it as the only authoritative rule of practice? Have we ever tried to live one day of our life so that it should resemble one of the days of the Son of Man? Knowing what He thought and did, and how He felt, have we ever tried to think and act and feel as He did—and if we have not, what wonder that our religion, being wholly theoretical, appears to us tainted with unreality, a thin-spun web of barren, fragile idealism which leaves us querulous and discontented?

Such a sense of discontent should be for us, as it really is, the signal of some deep mistake in our conception of religion. It should at least cause us alarm, for what can be more alarming than that we should be haunted with a sense of unreality in religion, yet still profess religion for reasons which leave the heart indifferent and barely serve to satisfy the intellect? And what can produce a keener torture in a sincere mind than this eternal suspicion of unreality in a religion whose conventional authority is acknowledged and accepted?

I am convinced that these feelings are general among great multitudes of the more thoughtful and intelligent adherents of

Christianity. Religion rests with them upon a certain intellectual acquiescence, or upon the equipoise of rational probabilities, or on the compromise of intellectual hesitations. Their tastes are gratified by the normal forms of worship, and their sentiments are softly stirred and stimulated. But when the voice of the orator dies upon the porches of the ear, and the music of the Church is silent, and the seduction of splendid ceremonial is forgotten, there remains the uneasy sense that between all this and the actual Carpenter-Redeemer there is a wide gulf fixed; that Jesus scarcely lived and died to produce only such results as these; that there must be some other method of interpreting His life, much simpler, much truer, and much more satisfying. Is it wonderful that among such men the current forms of Christianity excite no enthusiasm, and that the bonds of their attachment to it are lax and easily dissolved? And what is felt by these men within the Church is felt with much greater strength by multitudes of sincere men outside the Church, who do not hesitate to express their feeling and to pronounce current Christianity a burlesque and tragic travesty upon the real religion of the Nazarene.

But the moment we do begin to live, however inefficiently, as Jesus lived, the sublime reality of His religion is revealed to us. We do actually find that in the postponement of our own desires for the sake of others; in the abandonment of our own apparently legitimate ambitions for the service of the poor; in the patient endurance of affront and injury; in the forgiveness of those whose wrong seems inexpiable; in the daily exercise of love that "seeketh not itself to please," but hopeth all things, and believeth all things,—there is a joy beyond joy, and an exceeding great reward. We do actually find that to forgive our brother freely is better both for him and us than to judge him harshly, and the wisdom of Jesus is thus justified in its moral and social efficacy. We do actually find that in ceasing to live by worldly maxims and by living instead according to the maxims of Jesus, we have attained a form of happiness so incredibly sweet and pure that the world holds nothing that resembles it, and nothing that we would exchange for it. For this is now our great reward, that peace attends our footsteps, and that our hearts are no longer vexed with the perturbations of vanity and self-love, of envy and revenge. We find human nature answering to our touch even as it answered to the touch of Jesus, and revealing to us all its best and purest treasure. We find the very natures we thought intractable and destitute of all affinity with ours, brought near our own; the very men and women we thought wholly alien to us suddenly made lovable, and full of qualities that claim our love. And as we thus humbly follow in the steps of Jesus, trying to live each day as He lived, we know that sublimest joy of all—we feel Jesus acting once more through our actions, and we see in the eyes that meet our own the same look that Jesus saw in the eyes of those whom He had cured of misery and redeemed from sin.

A CONFESSION THE NOBLEST GRACE

'Tis something, when the day draws to its close,
To say, "Tho' I have borne a burdened mind,
Have tasted neither pleasure nor repose,
Yet this remains—to all men, friends or foes,
I have been kind."

'Tis something, when I hear Death's awful tread
Upon the stair, that his swift eye shall find
Upon my heart old wounds that often bled

For others, but no heart I injurèd—
    I have been kind.

Praise will not comfort me when I am dead;
Yet should one come, by tenderness inclined,
My heart would know if he stooped o'er my bed
And kissed my lips for memory, and said
    "This man was kind."

O Lord, when from Thy throne Thou judgest me,
Remember, tho' I was perverse and blind,
My heart went out to men in misery,
I gave what little store I had to Thee,
    My life was kind.

X
A CONFESSION

In speaking thus I do but speak of those things which have been revealed to me in my own experience. For many years I preached the truths of Christianity with a real sincerity, but with a fluctuating sense of their authority and value. Sometimes their authority seemed supreme, and then I trod on bright clouds high above the world; at other times they appeared to crumble at my touch, and then I walked in darkness. One thing I saw at intervals, and at last with complete and agonized distinctness, that however I preached these truths, they had little visible effect upon the lives of others. Those to whom I preached lived after all much as other people lived. I did not find them more magnanimous than the ordinary men and women of the world, nor less liable to take offense, to utter harsh words, to indulge in resentments, and to retaliate on those who injured them. I did not find that they loved humanity any better than their fellows; like all mankind they loved those who loved them, and had domestic virtues and affections, but little more. It was impossible to say that Christianity had produced in them any type of character wholly and radically different from that which might be found in multitudes of men and women who made no pretense of Christian sentiment. Christianity had no doubt imposed upon them many valuable restraints, so that without it they might have been worse men and women, but this was a merely negative result. Where was the spectacle of a character composed of new qualities, a life wholly governed by novel impulses and principles? I could not find such a life; nor ought I to have been surprised; for I could not find it in myself. I also lived much as other people did, except that I had a higher theory of conduct. Put to the test, I also showed resentment and was moved with the spirit of retaliation towards those who wronged me. Nor, save as a matter of theory and sentiment, did I love my fellows any better than the average of mankind. I sought those who were congenial to me, and had no pleasure in the company of the common and the ignorant. I liked clever people. I gave them my best, but I had nothing to bestow upon the dull and stupid. How many times have I borne the society of inferior people with ungracious tolerance, and hastened from them with undisguised relief? How often when dealing with the poor and ignorant in the exercise of conventional philanthropy, have I been careful to preserve the sense of a great gulf that yawned between me and them? And what was my daily life after all but a life existing for its own purposes, as most other men's lives were; and what credit could I take for the fact that the nature of those purposes was a trifle more consonant with what the world calls high ideals than theirs?

So the years went on, and the sense of unreality in my teaching grew steadily more intense and intolerable. I saw myself continually expending all the forces of my mind on theories which left me and my hearers alike unchanged in the essential characteristics of our lives. I felt myself, like St. Augustine, but a "seller of rhetoric." I was inculcating a method of life which I myself did not obey, or obeyed only in those respects that caused me neither sacrifice nor inconvenience. In order to continue such labours at all various forms of excuse and self-deception were required. Thus I flattered myself that I was at least maintaining the authority of morals. I did not perceive that morals are of no value to the world until vitalized by emotion. At other times I preached with strenuous zeal the superiority of the Christian religion, and dilated on its early triumphs. This pleased my hearers, for it always flatters men to find themselves upon the winning side. What I wonder at now is that they did not perceive that my zeal to prove Christianity true was exactly proportioned to my fear that it was false. Men do not seek to prove that of which they are assured. Jesus never sought to prove the existence of a God because He was assured of it; He simply asserted and commanded. In my heart of hearts I knew that I was not sure. But I did not easily discover the reason of my uncertainty. I supposed the source to be the destructive criticism of the Gospels which had reduced Jesus Himself to a probability. In my private thoughts I argued that it was no longer possible to feel the intense reality of Christ. Francis might feel it, Catherine might feel it, because they lived in an atmosphere of poetry, unchilled by criticism. I could never feel as they felt because I could not transport myself into their atmosphere. Yet as often as I turned to these great lives, something thrilled within me, some living responsive fibre, so that I knew that I was not after all quite alien to them. Could it be that there was that in me that made me, or could make me, of their company? But how could I attain to their faith? What could give back to a modern man, tortured by a thousand perplexities of knowledge of which they never dreamed, the reality of Christ which they possessed? And then the answer came—not suddenly, but as a still small voice slowly growing louder, more positive, more intense—*Live the Life*. Try to do some at least of the things that Jesus did. Seek through experience what can never come through ratiocination. *Be* a Francis; then it may be thou shalt think like him, and know Jesus as he knew Him. Live the life—there is no other way.

Simple and far from novel as the answer seems yet it came to me with the authority of a revelation. It illumined the entire circumference of life. I could no longer hesitate: Jesus had never spoken from the Syrian heavens more surely to the heart of Saul of Tarsus than He had to me. And in the moment that He spoke, I also, like Saul, found all my feelings altered, altered incredibly, miraculously, so that I scarcely recognized myself. I no longer stood aloof from men, and found pleasure in intellectual superiority; I was willing to "become a fool for Christ's sake" if by any means I might save some. I issued a card of invitation to the services of my Church with this motto of St. Paul's upon it, which I now felt was mine. I had had for years feelings of resentment towards one who I thought had wronged me; those feelings were now dead. In another case I had been harsh and unforgiving under great provocation; but when I met after a long interval of time, the one who had injured me, my heart had only love and pity for him. I sought out the drunkard and the harlot, and, when I found them, all repulsion perished in the flow of infinite compassion which I felt. I prayed with fallen women, sought them in their miserable abodes, fought with them for their own souls, and O exquisite moment!—I saw the soul awake in them, I saw in their tear-filled eyes the look that Jesus saw in the eyes of Magdalene. On my last Sabbath in London before leaving for America, one of these rescued girls, now as pure of look and manner as those most sweetly nurtured, called at my house to give my daughter a little present bought with the first money she had earned by honest toil in many years. On the day we sailed another said a special mass for us, and held the day sacred for prayer, in the convent where her bruised life had been nursed back to moral beauty. Love had triumphed in them, and I had brought them that love. I had lived the life, I had tried to do something that Jesus did, and behold Jesus had come back to me, and I knew His presence with me even as Francis knew it when he washed the leper's sores, and Catherine when she gathered to her bosom the murderer's guilty head, drew from him the confession of his sin, and whispered to him softly of the Lamb of God.

There is no sense of unreality in religion now for me. There are no weary uncertainties, no melancholy sense of beating the air in what I teach. He who will try to live the life of Jesus for a single day, and in such few particulars as may lie within his scope, will at once realize the presence of Jesus with him. In the practice of love comes the manifestation of the Lover, the drawing of the soul into the bosom of that Christ who was the very love of God, and the exchange of our poor proud carnal heart for the tender heart that yearned over Magdalene, was moved with compassion for the people, and broke upon the Cross.

A LOVER OF MEN

THE CRADLE CROSS

"What shall I ask for Thee, my child?"
Said Mary Mother, stooping dawn
Above the Babe all undefiled.
"O let Him wear a kingly crown."

From wise men's gifts she wrought the crown,
The robe inwove with many a gem,
Beside the Babe she laid them down.
He wept, and would have none of them.

"What shall I get for Thee, my Child?"
Unto the door she slowly went,
And wove a crown of thorn-boughs wild,
He took it up, and was content.

Upon the floor she gathered wood,
And made a little Cross for Him;
The Child smiled for He understood,
And Mary watched with eyes grown dim.

"Since these He doth prefer to gold,"
She sadly said, "Let it be so;
He sees what I cannot behold,
He knows what I can never know."

That night the eyes of Mary saw
A Cross of stars set in the sky,
Which after it the heavens did draw,
And this to her was God's reply.

XI
A LOVER OF MEN

When I recollect these experiences, and the almost breathless sense of joy which accompanied them, I can only marvel that I lived so many years without discovering the path that led to them. The path was quite plain, and nothing concealed it from me but my own pride. I could even see with distinctness those who trod it, not only the saints of far-off days, but men like Father Dolling, and women whose pale intense faces met mine from beneath the quaint ugliness of Salvation Army bonnets. These soldiers of the League of Service moved everywhere around me in the incessant processions of a tireless love. I knew their works, and there was no hour when my heart did not go out to them in sympathy. Why was it that I was only sympathizer and spectator, never comrade?

Partly through a kind of mischievous humility which was really pride. They could do these things; I could not, nor were they required of me. It needed special gifts for such a work, and I had not these gifts. Besides, had I not my own work? Was it not as important to educate persons of some culture and social position in a knowledge of Christian truth as to redeem lost people from the hell of their misdoing? Certainly it was easier and pleasanter. I found in it that most subtle of all gratifications, the sense of ability efficiently applied, and winning praise by its exertion. There was no one who wished me to live in any other way than that in which I lived. Those to whom I ministered were satisfied with me, and had I told them that I wished to do the sort of things that Salvation Army people did among the slums, they would have been shocked, and would certainly have dissuaded me. And so to this mischievous humility which assured me that I had no fitness for the kind of life which I knew was the life of the saints in every age, there was added the dull pressure of convention. Why should I do what no one expected me to do? Why could I not be content to fulfill the common standard approved by the average conception of Christianity?

I can see now how foolish and how wrong these thoughts were. I saw it even then at intervals. Again and again, like a torturing flash of fire, there ran through me illumining agonized dissatisfactions with myself, my work, my whole position. And again and again I let the flame die down, knowing not that the Son of Man had walked amid the fire. Nay more, I deliberately smothered the holy fire, being in part fearful of it, and of what its consequence might be, if once it were allowed to triumph. For I knew that if I followed these strange impulses my whole life must be changed, and I did not want it changed. I did not want to give up the ease of an assured position, the calm of studious hours, the tasks which flattered my ability. I did not want to face what I knew must happen, the estrangement of old friendships, the rupture of accustomed forms of life. Besides, I might be wholly wrong. I might have no real fitness for the tasks I contemplated; saints, like poets, were born, not made. No one who knew me would have believed me better fitted for any kind of life than that I lived. I had no friend who did not think my present life adequate and satisfactory, and many envied me for the good fortune that had given me just the kind of sphere which seemed best suited to me.

But now I see, as I look back, that at the root of all my inconsistency there lay this one thing, I was not a lover of my kind. I did not love men as men, humanity as humanity, as Jesus did. Of course I loved individuals, and even groups of men and classes of men, who could understand my thoughts, recognize my qualities, and repay my affection with affection. But to feel love for men as men; for those whose vulgarity distressed me, whose ignorance offended me, whose method of life repelled me; love for the drudge, the helot, the social pariah; love for people who had no beauty that men should desire them, nor any grace of mind or person, nor any quality that kindled interest; love for the dull average, with their painful limitations of mind and ideal, the gray armies of featureless grief, whose very sorrows had nothing picturesque in them and no tragic fascination—no, for these I had no real love. I had a deep commiseration, but it was that kind of romantic or aesthetic pity which begins and ends in its own expression. I did not know them by actual contact; I could not honestly say that I wished to know them. And then the thought came to me, and grew in me, that Jesus did love these people with an unconquerable passion. The multitudes to whom He preached were composed, as all multitudes are, of quite ordinary immemorable people. He also, to the eyes of those who saw Him in the peasant garb of Galilee, and judged only by outward appearance, was a common man. And so it would appear that if I did not love men after the fashion in which Jesus loved them, it was very unlikely that I should love Jesus Christ Himself if He once more appeared in the habit in which men saw Him long ago in Galilee. A Jesus, footsore, weary, travel-stained, wearing the raiment of a village carpenter, speaking with the accent of an unconsidered province, surrounded by a rabble of rude fishermen, among whom mingled many persons of doubtful character—how should I regard Him? Should I discern the Light and Life of men beneath His gray disguise of circumstance? Should I have left my books, my studious calm, my pleasant and sufficing tasks, to listen to One who seemed so little likely to instruct me? Would not the same spirit of disdain which made me think lightly and even scornfully of persons whose lives had no resemblance to my own, have made me disdainful of the Man of Nazareth? I knew the answer and I quailed before it. I saw that the temper of my mind was the temper of the Pharisee, and had I lived two thousand years ago in Jerusalem or Galilee, I should have rejected Jesus even as the scribes and Pharisees rejected Him.

And I should have rejected Him for the same reason, because I had no truly generous love of man as man. I should have been no better able to perceive than they that it had pleased God to clothe Himself in the flesh of one who united in His own person all those disabilities which incur the scorn of those who account themselves superior and cultivated, such as lowly and doubtful origin, poverty and the lack of liberal education, and methods of life which outraged social use and custom. Did not Jesus demand for the understanding of Himself precisely that temper which enabled Him to understand others, the temper which discerns the soul beneath all disguise of circumstance? He discerned the splendid and divine beneath the sordid. He saw beneath the drift of sin the buried magnificence of human nature as men discover the hidden temple beneath the sand-drift of the desert. He was able to love all men because all men were to Him living souls. And His own manifestation to the world was such that only those who had this temper could at all perceive His divine significance. The Pharisee could not see that significance simply because he was not accustomed to see men as men. He had no real interest in man as man. He was not a lover of his kind. Hence, when the Son of Man came out of Nazareth, the Pharisee was too careless or too supercilious to regard Him with interest. The divine wonder passed him by; all he saw was a wandering fanatic with no place to lay His head. He could not pierce the disguise of circumstance, and bow in love and awe before the soul of Jesus because he was not accustomed to discern the soul in common people. And so there came home to me the awful truth that I was not a lover of my kind. I was even as the Pharisees, and in denying my regard and love to the lowliest of men and women I was rejecting Jesus Christ. That which had seemed to me a strange exaggeration or an enigmatic sentence, now became a rational principle, a saying that had its root in the deep truth and reality of things; inasmuch as I showed not love to the least of these, my fellows, I denied my love to Jesus Christ Himself.

THE LAW OF COMPASSION

THE TRUE MUSIC

Not for the things we sing or say
He listens, who beside us stoops;
Too worn the feet, too hard the way,
Too sore the Cross wherewith He droops,
And much too great the need that cries
From these bruised eyelids and dim eyes.

He waits the water from the spring
Of kindness in the human heart,
The touch of hands, whose touches bring
A coolness to the wounds that smart,
The warm tears falling on His feet
Than precious ointment much more sweet.

O Lord, the way is hard and steep,
Help me to walk that way with Thee,
To watch with Thee, and not to sleep
Heedless of Thy Gethsemane,
Till love becomes my worshipping,
Who have no other gift to bring.

It is no hour for angel-harp,
The sky is dark, the Cross is near,

The agony of Death is sharp,
  The scorn of men upbraids Thine ear.
    Fain would I leave all empty creeds,
    And make a music of my deeds.

XII
THE LAW OF COMPASSION

Thus to love our fellow men is a difficult business,—there is none harder. It is so difficult that only a few in any age succeed on so conspicuous a scale as to attract prolonged attention. Yet the secret of success is not obscure; it lies in that temper of compassion which is the most beautiful of all features in the character of Jesus. When He looked upon the multitude He was "moved with compassion"—never was there more illuminative sentence. It reveals an attitude of mind absolutely original. For the general attitude towards the multitude in Christ's day was harsh and scornful. All the splendid intellectualism of Greece existed for the favoured few; beneath that glittering edifice of art and letters lay the dungeons of the slave. It was the same with Rome; it was an empire of privilege, in which the multitude had no part. Jewish society was built after the same pattern, except that with the Pharisee the sense of religious superiority bred a kind of arrogance much more bitter than that which is the fruit of intellectual or social exclusiveness. With men of this temper the call to love all men as fellows could only provoke anger and derision. What possible relation could exist between an Athenian philosopher and a helot, a Roman noble and a slave, a Pharisee proud of his meticulous knowledge of the law, and the common people who were unlettered? The gulf that yawned between such lives was as wide as that which separates the scholar, the artist, or the aristocrat of modern Europe from the pale toiler of a New York sweating-room, or the coal carriers of Zanzibar or Aden. When Jesus bade the young ruler sell all that he had and give it to the poor, He proposed an entirely unthinkable condition of discipleship. He bade him discard all the privileges of his order. He proposed instead real comradeship with the poor, He Himself being poor. For two thousand years the pulpit has denounced the young ruler for not doing what no one even now would think of doing—not even those who are most eloquent in denunciation.

We may waive the question of whether the advice of Jesus to the young ruler was meant to be of particular or universal application, but we cannot ignore the new law of life which Jesus formulated when He made compassion the supreme social virtue. For it is only through compassion that we learn to understand those who differ from us in social station or temperament, and can at all come to love them. Let me examine my own natural tendencies, and I am soon made aware of how impossible it is to love *all* my fellow men. I commence my life, for instance, under conditions which permit me to see only a small section of society, which I imagine to be the world itself. I know nothing, and am told nothing, of those whose lives do not lie in the direct line of my limited vision. The process of education removes me at each stage further from the likelihood of knowing them. I acquire ideals, habits, and manners of which they are destitute. I come to regard an acquaintance with various forms of knowledge as essential to life, and I am naturally disdainful of those who do not possess this knowledge. In the same way I regard a certain code of manners as binding, and the lack of this code of manners in others as an outrage. My very thoughts have their own dialect, and I am totally unacquainted with the dialect of those whose thoughts differ from my own. Thus with the growth of my culture there is the equal growth of prejudice; with the enjoyment of my privilege, a tacit rejection and repudiation of the unprivileged.

How then am I ever to find myself in any relation of affection towards these human creatures from whom I am alienated by the nature of my education? If, by any chance, I come in contact with them, it is certain that they will arouse in me repugnance and perhaps disgust. I shall find them coarse, crude, and ignorant; their methods of speech will grate upon me, their manners will repel me; they will be as truly foreign to me as the natives of New Guinea, and their total incapacity to share the thoughts which compose my own inner life will be scarcely less complete. It is a truly humiliating thing to admit that differences of nationality separate men less effectually than disparity of manners. If I am at all fastidious I am more likely to be repelled by coarse language, gross habits, or vulgar behaviour in my fellow mortal than by all his errors in creed or morals. So little parts men, and is permitted to part them, that it is very likely that some mere awkwardness of behaviour in my fellow man may extirpate effectually the regard I might have had for him. How little indeed is permitted to part friends—often nothing more than a tone of voice, a word misinterpreted, or something equally slight, the product very possibly of shyness, or inability for right expression on a sudden call. And there is all that goes by the name of antipathy, the nameless and quite irrational repulsions which we permit ourselves to cherish, for which we have no better excuse than that they are instinctive. With all these forces against us how can we love our neighbour as ourselves? It is something if we do not detest him; if we tolerate him it should be counted to us for a virtue.

Yet the method by which we may love him is quite simple; it is to approach him not with judgment but compassion, to put ourselves in his place, to see his life from his point of view instead of our own. What is his ignorance after all but lack of opportunity? What are his bad manners but the penalty of a narrow life? What are these habits of his which so offend me but things inevitable in that condition of servitude which he occupies—a servitude, let me recollect, which ministers to my ease and comfort? To-day, not less than in earlier generations, society resembles the palaces of the Italian Renaissance,—the feast of life in the painted hall, and the groaning of the prisoner in the depths below. For every comfort that I have, some one has sweated. My fire is lit not only with coal from the mine, but with the miner's flesh and blood; my food has come through roaring seas in which men perished by hurricane and shipwreck; the very books from which I draw my culture are the product not alone of the scholar and the thinker, but of rude unlettered men in forest and at forge who helped to make them by their toil. If I were as educated as I claim to be I should know myself debtor to the barbarian as truly as to the Greek, and as I read my book I should see the forest falling that it might be woven into paper, and men labouring in the heat of factories that the moulded metal might become the organ of intelligence. Nay, I should see yet more; for would it not appear that these nameless toilers are richer in essential life, and in the deep knowledge of what man's existence is, than even the scholar and the writer, whose main acquaintance with life is with words rather than acts? They toil with tense muscles through the summer heat and winter cold; they endure hardship and danger; and week by week their scanty wage is shared by wives and children, who excite in them tenderness and self-sacrifice, and repay them with affection and devotion. For it is so decreed that the sacred magnanimities of the human heart come to flower as fully in lives of crude labour as in lives of ease; these roughened hands grow gentle when they touch the heads of little children, on these strong breasts the wife rests her weariness, and these lips that speak a language so different from mine have nevertheless known the sacramental wine of love. Were my life weighed with theirs might it not appear that theirs was the richer in essential fortitude, in patience and endurance, in all the final qualities that compose the finest manhood?

The spirit of compassion interprets these lives to me; it lends me vision. It enables me to see them not in their artificial disparities, but in their deep-lying kinship with mine and all other lives. And the same thing happens when I survey lives stained with folly, wrecked by weakness, or made detestable by sin and crime. I also have known folly, weakness, sin; but for me there were compulsions to a virtuous life which these never knew. Why am I not as these? Perhaps because my nature rests on a securer equipoise, or because there is in it a certain power of moral recuperation which these have lacked, or because I have the prudence that stops short of consummated folly, or because my environment imposes and creates restraint, or because I have never known the peculiar violence of temptation before which they succumbed. There may be a hundred reasons, but scarce one which gives me cause for boasting. With their life to live, had I done better? Exposed to their temptations, deprived of all the helpful friendships that have interposed between my life and ruin, should I have done as well? In those wakeful hours of night when all my past life runs before me like a frieze of flame, how clearly do I see how frequently I grazed the snare, hung over gulfs of wild disaster, courted ruin, and escaped I know not how? Remembering this, can I be hard towards those who fell? Can I pride myself on an escape in which my will had little part, a deliverance which was a kind of miracle, wrought not by virtue or discretion, but by some outside force which thrust out a strong and willing hand to save me? And, as these thoughts pursue me, I find myself all at once regarding these wrecked and miserable lives not from the outside but the inside. I penetrate their inmost coil of being, and see with horror the crumbling of the house of life—with horror, but also with a torturing pity. And then because compassion lives in me, I can at last separate between the sinner and his sin. The sin remains abhorrent, but I cannot hate the sinner. I see him as one who has fallen in a bad cause, but his wounds cry so loud for pity that I forget the moral treason that has brought him to a battle-field so ignominious and so disastrous. And out of the pity grows love, for love is the natural end of pity; and the magnanimity of love, overleaping moral values, fixes only on the fact of suffering that appeals for succour, misery that cries for help. This was the vital fact that Jesus saw when He had compassion on the multitude.

Jesus had compassion on the multitude, and He gives the reason; He saw them as sheep having no shepherd. It was the element of misdirection in their lives on which Jesus fixed His glance—it was for lack of guidance and a shepherd they had gone astray. May not the same be said of all the lives that fail, whether through ignorance or want, folly or crime? Rightly guided they might have attained knowledge and esteem, wisdom and virtue; and if that be so, no man of right spirit can refuse to feel the pathos of their situation. It is to this point that Jesus leads us. He makes us conscious of "the still sad music of humanity." No further incentive is needed to make us love humanity than the pathos of the human lot. A man may be a knave, a fool, a rogue; yet could we unravel all the secrecies of his disaster we should find so much to move our pity, so much in his life which resembles crises in our own, that in the end the one vision that remains with us is of a wounded brother man. When once we see that vision all our pride of virtue dies in us, and quicker yet to die is the temper of contempt which we have nurtured towards those whose faults offend us. A yet greater offense is ours if we can behold suffering, however caused, without pity. Worse than the worst crime which man can commit against society, or the worst personal wrong he can inflict on us, is the temper in ourselves which judges him without mercy, and refuses him the one medicine that may reinvigorate him—the balm of pity and forgiveness. And, after all, of what wrong is it not true that the bitterest suffering it creates falls not upon the wronged but the wronger, so that in the end the sinner is the real victim, and like all victims should be the object of compassion rather than of vengeance?

THE EMPIRE OF LOVE

THE WOMAN WHO WAITED

She wrought warm garments for the poor,
  From morn to eve unwearied she
Went with her gifts from door to door;
  And when the night drew silently
Along the streets, and she came home,
She prayed, "O Lord, when wilt Thou come?"

She was but loving, she could please
  With no rare art of speech or song.
The art she knew was how to ease
  The sick man's pain, the weak man's wrong;
And every night as she came home
She said, "O Lord, when wilt Thou come?"

The truths men praised she deemed untrue,
  The light they hailed to her was dim,
But that the Christ was kind she knew,
  She knew that she must be like Him.
Like Mary, in her darkened home,
She sighed, "O Christ, that thou would'st come!"

Her hair grew white, her house was bare,
Yet still her step was firm and glad,
The feet of Hunger climbed the stair,
For she had given all she had.
She died within her empty home
Still seeking One who did not come.

She rose from out the wave of death,
A Stranger stood beside the shore;
The robe she wrought with failing breath,
And staining tears, the Stranger wore.
He drew her tired heart with His smile,
"Lo, I was with thee all the while."

XIII
THE EMPIRE OF LOVE

But if this spirit of compassion were general, would virtue itself be secure? Would not a fatal lenience towards vice become the temper of society? Would not the immediate effect be the declaration of a general amnesty towards every kind of wrong-doer, and from such an act what could be expected but a rapid dissolution of the laws and conventions that maintain the structure of society?

These are natural fears, and they are not altogether the fears of weak and timid men. They will certainly be shared by all tyrants, all persons whose tempers incline to absolutism, all believers in force as the true dynamic of stable social government. To reason with such persons is impossible, because their opinions are the fruit of temper, and are therefore irrational. But even such persons are not destitute of powers of observation, and in the long history of the world there is a field of observation which no person of intelligence can neglect.

Do we find, as we survey this field, that force has ever proved the true dynamic of stable social government? We find the exact contrary to be true. The great empires of the past were founded on force and perished, even as Napoleon discovered in his final reveries on human history. Whenever force has been applied to maintain what seemed a right social system it has uniformly failed. The Church of Rome applied force to produce a world consonant with her ideas of truth; she was all but destroyed by the recoil of her prolonged persecutions. The Puritans were persecuted in the name of truth and virtue; they triumphed. The Puritans in turn persecuted, under the impulse of ideals that an impartial judgment must pronounce among the loftiest and noblest that ever animated human hearts, and in turn they were overthrown. Again and again, when crime has attained monstrous and threatening proportions, laws of barbarous severity have been applied for its repression; in not one solitary instance have they been successful. The more barbarous and severe the law against crime, the more has crime flourished. When men were hanged for petty theft, when they were whipped at the cart's tail for seditious language, when they were disembowelled for treasonable practices; theft, sedition, and treason flourished as they have never flourished since. The very disproportion and hideousness of the penalty inflamed men's minds to the commission of wrong. On the contrary, the birth of lenience and humanity was immediately rewarded by a decline of crime. These are lessons which we do well to recollect to-day when statesmen advocate the death penalty for the anarchist, irrespective of his exact crime; when city councils propose the same penalty for those guilty of outrages on women; when indignant mobs, in spite of law, and without trial, burn at the stake offending negroes. If history teaches anything with an emphasis at once clear and unmistakable, it is that crime has never yet been abridged by brutal harshness, but has thriven on it. History also teaches with an emphasis equally clear and positive, that the spirit of love, manifesting itself in lenience, compassion, and magnanimity, has constantly justified itself by the reduction of crime, and the taming of the worst kind of criminal.

Is not this in itself a justification of the spirit of Jesus? Does it not appear, on the review of nearly two thousand years of history, that society has attained its greatest happiness and has reached its highest condition of virtue, precisely in those periods when the gentle ideals of Jesus have had most sway over human thought and action? And if this be so, is it possible to doubt that society will only continue to progress towards happiness and content in the degree that it obeys the counsels of Jesus, making not force but love the great social dynamic, which shall control all its operations and guide all its judgments?

It may appear impossible and inexpedient for the human judge to say to the offender, "Neither do I condemn thee; go, sin no more"; but it is very clear that the opposite course does by no means lead to a cessation of sin. For what is the total result of all our punishments in the name of law but the manufacture of criminals? According to our theory of punishment a jail should be a seminary of virtue and reformation. Men submitted to its discipline should come out new creatures, cured of every tendency to crime. On the contrary, in nine cases out of ten, they come out a thousandfold worse than they went in. If this is not the case, it is because some Christian influence, not included in our legal system, has reached them. But such influences reach very few. The influences that operate in the great majority of cases are wholly demoralizing. Those who enter a jail with genuine intentions of reform speedily discover that they are not expected to reform. They are branded indelibly. They are exposed to the corruption of associates a hundredfold worse than themselves. They leave the jail with every avenue of honest industry closed to them, every man's hand against them, and no career possible to them but a life of crime. When we consider these things we have little cause to congratulate ourselves upon the results of our systems of justice. Even a general amnesty towards every form of crime could scarcely produce results more deplorable. Fantastic as it may appear, yet it seems not improbable that the abolition of the jail and of all penal law, might produce benefits for humanity such as centuries of punishment on crime have wholly failed to produce.

But no one asks this at present, though the day may come sooner than we think, when society, tired of the long failure and absolute futility of all its attempts to cleanse the world of crime by penal enactments, will make this demand. It is enough now if we press the question whether there is not good ground in all this dreary history of futility and failure, to make some attempt to govern society by the ideals of Jesus? Why should not the Church replace the jail? Why should not the offender be handed over to a company of Christian people, instead of a company of jailers, paid to be harsh, and by the very nature of their occupation trained to harsh tempers and cruel acts? Who are better fitted for the custody of the criminal than people whose lives are based on the merciful ideals of Jesus? How could such persons be better employed than in devoting themselves to the restoration of self-respect in the fallen, than in the attempt to nurture into vigour his bruised or dormant instincts of right, than in the organized effort to restore him to some place in society which should give him honest bread in return for honest labour? Few men are criminals by choice. Crime is more often the fruit of weakness than intention. Almost every criminal would prefer an honourable life if he knew how to set about it. Can we doubt that if Jesus presided in the councils of His Church to-day, this would be one of the first directions in which He would apply His energy? And who that surveys the modern Church with undeflected judgment would not say that the Church would be a thousand times dearer to the world, a thousand times more sacred, respected, and authoritative, if instead of spending its time in spiritual self-gratification, and its riches in the adornment of its worship, it became the true

Hospice of the Fallen and Unfortunate, thus exemplifying in its action that love for men which was the essential spirit of its Founder?

It will no doubt be replied that the Church already, by a thousand institutions, of a philanthropic character, is attempting this very work. But this is an evasion of the point, for such institutions only begin their work of redemption when the existing social systems have accomplished their work of destruction. Moreover, no institution, however admirable, can be a substitute for the general action of the Church. It is precisely this practice of substitution that accounts for so much of the weakness of the Church. It is so much more easy and pleasant to devolve upon others duties which to us are disagreeable, to buy ourselves out of the conscription of personal duty, to persuade ourselves that we have done all that can be asked of us when we have given money for some worthy end, that it is not surprising that multitudes of excellent and kindly people adopt such views and practices. But, in doing so, they miss not only the joy of personal well-doing, but also the sense of reality in the good that is done. And the spectator and critic of the life of the Church, although he may not be ignorant of the kind of work done by these institutions, nevertheless is keenly conscious of the lack of reality in the work of the Church, when he finds that its individual members are leading lives in no way distinguishable by any active love for their fellows. For the main reason why thoughtful men manifest aversion to the Church is not found in dislike for her worship, or rejection of her creeds; it is found rather in the sense of unreality in her life. Who, such men will ask, among all this multitude of well-dressed worshippers, offering their adoration to the Deity, visits the fatherless and widow in their affliction, lays restraining hands upon the tempted, uplifts the fallen or instructs the depraved, and so fulfills the true ideal of religion pure and undefiled? What is the exact nature of their impact upon society? Are they more merciful, more compassionate, more sympathetic than average mankind? Do they not share the same social prejudices, and guide their lives by the same social traditions as the bulk of men and women? And if nothing more than this can be predicated of them, how is it possible to avoid that impression of essential unreality which is inseparable from the subscription to social ideals infinitely loftier and purer than any others in human history, united with lives which in no way rise above the average? Here is the true reason why thoughtful men think lightly, and even scornfully of the Church. It is not the truths and ideals of Jesus that offend them, but the travesty of those truths and ideals in the average life of Christians.

But whenever any man attempts to live in the spirit of Jesus, the first to rally to him are the sincere recusants from the church. He may be satirised, and probably will be, as a moral anarchist, a fanatic, and a hare-brained enthusiast; but nevertheless the best men will rally to him. They rallied to a Father Dolling, they rally to a General Booth. The types represented by such men lie far apart. One was so high a ritualist as to be almost Catholic, the other is an ecclesiastic anarchist so extreme that he dispenses with the sacraments. But these things count for little; what the world sees in such men is the essential reality of their life. One of the severest critics of Dolling once went to hear him with the bitterest prejudice. He found him with a couple of hundred thieves and prostitutes gathered round him, to whom he was telling the love of Jesus in the simplest language. "Dolling may be a Roman Catholic, or anything else he pleases," said his critic; "all I know is that I never heard any one speak of Christ like that," and from that hour he was his warmest friend. No doubt similar conversions of sentiment have attended the ministries of all apostolic men and women, of Francis and Catherine, of Wesley and Whitfield, of Moody and General Booth. Men know by instinct the lover of his kind. Men forgive a hundred defects for the sake of reality. Perhaps the sublimest of all justifications of Christ's law of love is that no man has truly practiced it in any age without himself rising into a life of memorable significance, without immediate attestations of its virtue in the transformation of society, without attracting to himself the reverence and affection of multitudes of fellow workers who have rendered him the same adoring discipleship that the friends of Jesus gave to Him.

No doubt it will also be said that were the ideals thus indicated to triumph, there would be nothing left for the direction of society but a mischievous and sentimental spirit of amiability. The general fibre of virtue would disintegrate. Pity for the sinner, pushed to such extremes, would in the end mean tolerance for sin. But to such an objection the character of Jesus furnishes its own reply. The character of Jesus displays love in its supreme type, but it is wholly lacking in that weak-featured travesty of love which we call amiability. His hatred of sin was at times a furious rage. His lips breathed flame as well as tenderness; "Out of His mouth proceeded a sharp two-edged sword." We may search literature in vain to discover any words half as terrible and scathing as the words in which Jesus described sin. The psychological explanation is that great powers of love are twin with great powers of hatred. The passionate love of virtue is, in its obverse, an equally passionate hatred of vice. In the same way the passionate love of our kind has for its obverse an equally passionate hatred for the wrongs they endure. For this reason justice and virtue are nowhere so secure as in the hands of men who love their kind intensely. They are most insecure in the hands of the cynic, who despises his kind, and therefore misapprehends their conduct. For love, in its last analysis, is understanding, and where there is understanding of our fellows there can hardly fail to be wisdom in our method of treating them. That was the great secret of Jesus in these examples which we have reviewed. He understood Simon Peter. He understood the woman who was a sinner. He therefore knew the only wise method of treating them. One with less pity might have sent the harlot back to her shame, one with less love might have driven Peter into permanent apostasy. But Jesus, in His understanding of the human heart, knew the exact limit of reproof, the exact point at which magnanimity became efficacious in redemption. Those who follow His spirit will attain the same rare wisdom. They will never sacrifice virtue to compassion, nor will they put virtue in opposition to compassion. One question may suffice. Would we be content to leave the administration of society in the hands of Jesus? Would we confidently submit our own case to His jurisdiction? If, in every dispute between men and nations, in every case of wrong and crime, Jesus were the one Arbiter, would the world be better ruled, would the probable course of events be such as to increase the sum of human happiness? We can scarcely hesitate in the reply—we, who daily pray that His kingdom may come. And if to such questions we return our inevitable affirmative, we cannot doubt that society has everything to gain in being governed by those who live most closely in the spirit of Jesus; that they, and they only, are the true leaders and judges of the nations.

THE BUILDERS OF THE EMPIRE

THE PRAYER

Lover of souls, indeed,
  But Lover of bodies too,
Seeing in human flesh
  The God shine through;
Hallowed be Thy name,
  And, for the sake of Thee,
Hallowed be all men,
  For Thine they be.

Doer of deeds divine,
  Thou, the Father's Son,
In all Thy children may
  Thy will be done,
Till each works miracles
  On poor and sick and blind,
Learning from Thee the art
  Of being kind.

For Thine is the glory of love,
  And Thine the tender power,
Touching the barren heart
  To leaf and flower,
Till not the lilies alone,
  Beneath Thy gentle feet,
But human lives for Thee
  Grow white and sweet.

And Thine shall the Kingdom be,
  Thou Lord of Love and Pain,
Conqueror over death
  By being slain.
And we, with the lives like Thine
  Shall cry in the great day when

Thou earnest to claim Thine own,
"All Hail! Amen."

XIV
THE BUILDERS OF THE EMPIRE

It may be long before the world recognizes this leadership of the loving, and accepts their judgment, but nevertheless the world is debtor to them for all that sweetens life, and makes society tolerable. Such men and women move unrecognized, doing their kindly work without praise, and not so much as asking praise from men; but theirs is a securer triumph than earth can give, and on their brows rests a rarer crown than earthly monarchs wear. I know many of these men and women, and I never meet them without the sense that the seamless robe of Christ has touched me. I meet them in unlikely places; I overtake them on the road of life, oftenest in the places where the shadows lie most thickly; but on each brow is the white stone which is the sign of peace, and in each voice is that deep note of harmony that belongs alone to those who walk through tribulations which they overcome, griefs of which they know the meaning, sorrows which they have the skill to heal. Their very footsteps move more evenly than other men's, as though guided by the rhythm of a music others do not hear; their very hands have a softness only known to hands that bind up wounds and wipe men's tears away; and in all their movements and their aspect is a stillness and a sweet composure, as of hearts at rest. Whence are these, and why are they arrayed in white robes? And we know the answer, though no angel-voice may speak to us; these are they on whose bowed heads the starlight of Gethsemane has fallen, in whose hands are the wounds of service, in whose breasts is the heart that breaks with love for men.

One such man I met some months ago, fresh from the forests of Wisconsin. Through a long spring day he told me his story, or rather let me draw it from him episode by episode, for he was much too modest to suppose anything that he had done remarkable. After wild and careless years of wasted youth, Christ had found him, and from the day of his regeneration he gave himself to the redemption of his fellow men. He became a "lumber-jack," a preacher to the rough sons of the Wisconsin forests. He told me how he first won their respect by sharing their toil—he, a fragile slip of a man, and they giants in thew and muscle: how by tact and kindness he got a hearing for his Master; how he travelled scores of miles through the winter snows to nurse dying men, wrecked by wild excesses; how he had sat for hours together with the heads of drunken men, on whom the terror had fallen, resting on his knees, performing for them offices of help which no other would attempt; how he had heard the confessions of thieves and murderers, who had fled from justice to the refuge of the forest; how he had stood pale, and apprehensive of violence in an angry drunken mob, and had quelled their rage by singing to them "Anywhere with Jesus"; how, finally, he had fallen ill, and had hoped in his extreme weariness for the great release, but had come back from the gates of death with a new hope for the success of his work; and as he spoke, that light which fell upon the face of the dying Stephen rested also on his face; for he also saw, and made me see, the heavens opened, and Jesus standing at the right hand of the throne of God. He was only a lumber-jack, but to these men he was a Christ. He was poor, so poor, that I marvelled how he lived; but he had adopted into his home the forsaken child of a drunken lumberman, whose wife was dead. His life was full of hardship, but never have I met a happier man. For he had found the one secret of all noble and tranquil living, the life of service; and as I grasped his hand at parting and remembered how often it had rested in healing sympathy upon the evil and the weary, I thought of the words of the blessed Master, "He laid His hands upon her, and the fever left her, and she rose and ministered unto Him."

Another man of the same order I have talked with as these concluding lines were written. He had begun life with brilliant prospects as a lawyer, had been wrecked by drink, and one night while drunk had fallen overboard into deep water, and had with difficulty been brought back to life. From that hour his life was changed. He went to a Western city and became a missionary to drunkards and harlots. He told me of a youth of nineteen he had recently visited in prison. The youth was a murderer, and the woman he had loved had committed suicide. He was utterly impervious to reproof, did not want to live, and said that if his mistress had gone to hell he wanted to go there too, for she was the only human creature who had ever loved him. "God loves you," said my friend; "yes, and I love you too. I know how you feel. You want just to be loved. Come, my poor boy, let me love you." And at that appeal this youth, with triple murder on his conscience, melted, and flung his arms round the neck of his visitor, and sobbed out all the story of his sin and shame. O exquisite moment when the heart melts at the touch of love—could all the heaped-up gains of a life of pleasure or ambition yield such felicity as this? For this man's face, rough and plain as it was, glowed as he spoke with the same light that beatified the features of my friend the lumber-jack—"the Lord God gave them light," and the Lamb upon the throne was the light of all their seeing.

A little while ago to this man came the offer of restoration to the social place which he has lost. He might have gone back to his forfeited career, with an ample income. He put the case to his wife and to his boys; with instant unanimity they said, "Never;

this work is the best work in the world." And so the once brilliant lawyer is happy on a pittance, happier than he ever could be on a fortune, because he is doing Christ's work of love among his fellow men. And these instances are typical. In every corner of the world are those who belong to the true Society of Jesus—the Order of Love and Service,—and the happiest lives lived on earth are lived by these men and women. For Jesus will not suffer any man to be the loser by Him; He overpays those who truly follow Him with a happiness that worlds could not buy; and "even in the present time," so enriches with the love of others those who love, that they are unconscious of any deprivation in their lot, knowing in all things, amid poverty, insult, violence, hardship and pain, that their gain exceeds their loss by measureless infinitudes of joy.

We may be neither wise nor great, but we may be loving, and he who loves is already "born of God, and knoweth God, for God is love." We may have but a poor understanding of conflicting theologies and philosophies, and may even find our minds hostile to accepted creeds; but we can live lives of pitiful and serviceable love. He who does these things is the true Christian and no other is. Against the man who loves his fellows Heaven cannot close its doors, for He who reigns in Heaven is the Lover of men, and the greatest Lover of them all. We know now why He is loved as no other has been loved. We know now what His religion truly is; it is the religion of Love. To accept this religion requires in us but one quality, the heart of the little child which retains the freshness and obeys the authority of the emotions; but unless we become as little children we cannot enter this kingdom. This is the condition of entrance, and the method is equally simple. It is to follow Jesus in all our acts and thoughts, to allow no temper that we do not find in Him, to build our lives upon His ideals of love and justice, remembering always that He is more than the Truth,—He is the Way in which men may confidently tread, and the Life which they may share.

All things in the intellectual and social life of men move, as by a fixed law, towards simplification. May we not hope that this same tendency may permeate the universal Church of Christ, dissolving the accretions of mistaken and conventional piety, combining the vital elements into a new synthesis, at once simple and convincing,—the new which is the oldest and the earliest,—that the Church is the organ of the Divine Love, and that love alone is the Christian equivalent of religion?

May we not even anticipate that the visible decay of many symbols that once were authoritative, of many forms of creed that are now barely tolerated rather than respected, may work towards this issue; that gradually the test of service will supplant the test of intellectual belief, and that a new Church will arise founded not on creed at all, but on a real imitation of the life of Jesus? If this should happen we need not regret the dissolution of the forms of religious life which is so evident to-day, for though the older kingdom be shaken, we shall arrive in God's time at the better kingdom which cannot be shaken.

When the Church does manifestly become the organ of the Divine Love, visibly creating a type of loving and lovable men and women found nowhere else, whose lives are as lamps borne before the feet of the weary and the lost, then the world, now hostile or indifferent to the Church, will love the Church even as by instinct it loves the Christ. Such lives have been lived, and they are, even to those who have the least instinct for religion, the most sacred memories of history, and the most inspiring.

Such lives may still be lived by all who love the Lord Christ Jesus in sincerity.

www.ingramcontent.com/pod-product-compliance
Lightning Source LLC
LaVergne TN
LVHW021943220826
846092LV00010B/1214

9789354787317